BEST
PUB WALKS
IN THE
NORTH PENNINES

Nick Channer

Published by Sigma Leisure – an imprint of
Sigma Press, 1 South Oak Lane, Wilmslow, Cheshire SK9 6AR, England.

British Library Cataloguing in Publication Data
A CIP record for this book is available from the British Library.

ISBN: 1-85058-413-3

Typesetting and Design by: Sigma Press, Wilmslow, Cheshire.

Front cover: The Stag Inn, Dufton

All photographs by: Nick Channer

Maps by: Jeremy Semmens

Printed by: Manchester Free Press

Disclaimer: the information in this book is given in good faith and is believed to be correct at the time of publication. No responsibility is accepted by either the author or publisher for errors or omissions, or for any loss or injury howsoever caused. You must judge your own fitness, competence and experience.

Preface

I think I must have inherited my love for the great outdoors from my parents. When I was a child I travelled virtually everywhere on foot as we did not possess a car. This, I think, fostered in me a love of walking and the countryside, as well as helping me, in later life, to forge a career as an 'outdoor journalist'. How successful I can claim to be in this field is debatable, but what is certain is that all that enforced childhood activity has given me a healthy constitution, a sturdy pair of legs and a liking for real ale!

On reaching my teens, it wasn't long before I was captivated by the spellbinding beauty of Northern England, the true playground of the outdoor enthusiast. Being a keen hill walker, it had always seemed a logical step to head north. Over the years I have made countless trips to the wilds of Yorkshire, the Lake District and Scotland, but the rugged landscapes of the North Pennines were new to me. It was when I came to write a book of lesser-known long-distance treks, that I first discovered the unique and special character of this region. That was a few years ago and since then I have been drawn back again and again to Britain's largest Area of Outstanding Natural Beauty – dubbed "England's Last Wilderness" by the botanist David Bellamy. The label may have been adopted by the tourist boards and the marketing men, anxious to promote the region after its AONB status was conferred by the Countryside Commission in 1988, but the description is certainly apt.

This is Britain at its wildest and beautiful best – 772 square miles of spectacular ravines, green dales, hills, forest and high moorland sandwiched between four of our National Parks – the Lake District, Yorkshire Dales, North York Moors and Northumberland. A few weeks spent in the North Pennines working on this book has confirmed to me beyond any doubt that the pace of life is slow and unhurried, the roads are comparatively traffic free compared with other areas – it was some time before I realised I hadn't seen a traffic light – the scenery is magnificent, the weather is changeable and erratic, but, most important of all, the beer is cheap. For me, the timeless Pennines have a spiritual quality. On summer days I have often lost all sense of time as I gazed down from my splendid viewpoint at the empty green world below. There is something marvellously therapeutic about such an exercise, something so restful and soothing. Walking in these hills allows you to escape the reality of the modern world, restoring a sense of peace and well-being. The North Pennines, in particular, provide us with a unique natural playground, an outdoor museum where, apart from the magnificent views, the numerous walks across the roof of England and the chance to sample the beauty and the fresh air, we can learn so much about our natural history and industrial heritage.

At the risk of sounding a bit of a moralist, I feel I must add my voice to the calls for care, protection and preservation in the North Pennine countryside. We may have access to the hills and the lonely moorland, but we must treat this matchless region of Britain with the respect it deserves. Finally, my thanks to Jane Brantom and her colleagues at the North Pennines Tourism Partnership for their patience and assistance, and all those people, including landlords and hoteliers, who were so helpful and made me so welcome during the preparation of this book.

Nick Channer

CONTENTS

Introduction

The Walks

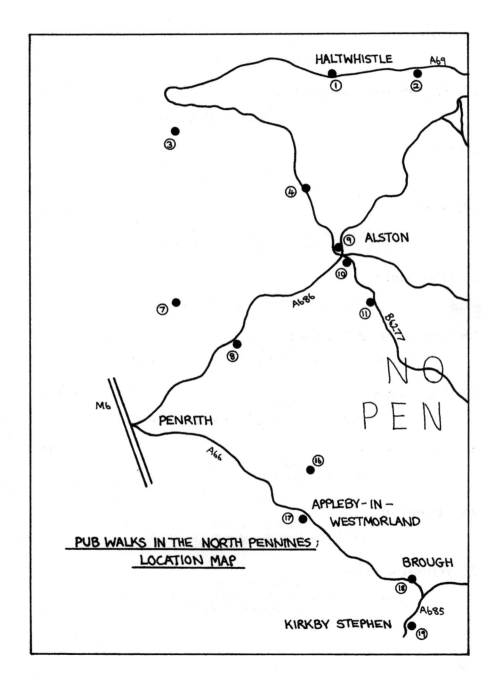

PUB WALKS IN THE NORTH PENNINES ;
LOCATION MAP

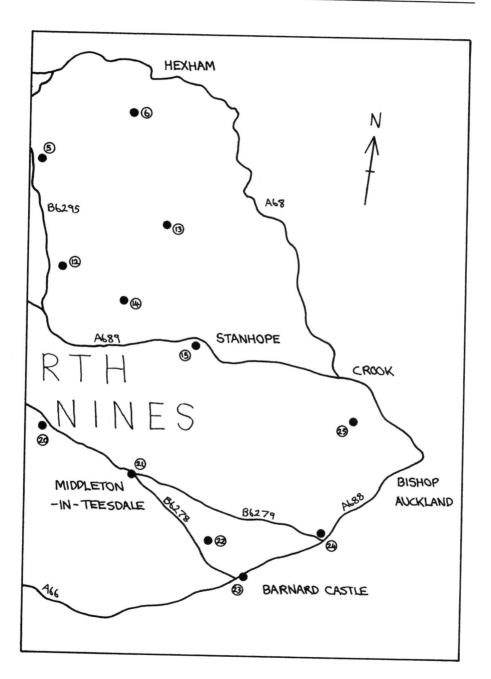

Introduction

There are so many things that make "England's Last Wilderness" a special and unique region of the country. Apart from the breathtaking scenery, for which it is most famous, the area abounds with evidence of ancient legends and myths and age-old cultures.

The Pennine Way, which runs north to south through the heart of the hills, has helped to generate popularity over the years but despite the obvious attractions, the North Pennines have long been one of the least-visited parts of the country. Many people – visitors and locals alike – have always welcomed the peace and solitude of these unpopulated upland landscapes, protective of their magical aura. Others, perhaps more reliant on the influx of tourism, have eagerly tried to encourage signs of commercial exploitation. Perhaps for too long overshadowed by the nearby National Parks, the region is at last beginning, if a little cautiously, to emerge from its shell, accommodating the needs and demands of the tourist industry, asserting itself as truly the last wilderness. For many years the North Pennines catered mainly for backpackers on the Pennine Way, with a limited range of small inns and hotels. These days the choice is altogether more sophisticated, aimed at the more discerning visitor and holidaymaker.

Much of what you see in the North Pennines is influenced by the elements. The weather, merciless and uncompromising, shapes the landscape and there is no better example of how it does this than in the cold climate of Northern England. Often covered in snow for much of the year – even in early summer the summits are still flecked with snow – the glorious North Pennines are home to a variety of artists, writers and photographers, many of whom have moved here from the south in search of solitude and inspiration. They certainly find it high among these windswept hills. Even Turner and Sir Walter Scott were moved to celebrate the area in their work. Many of the individuals I have met in the North Pennines are adopted 'Pennine people' – mostly southerners whose love for the area is such that they have vowed never to leave.

The North Pennines region has its own distinctive culture. Its inhabitants are a mixture of locals whose ties with the hills can be traced back over generations and who are employed mainly in local farming. Many are newcomers to the area and have launched their own businesses. This is crucial to the success of the local economy, helping shopkeepers to survive and schools to stay open – among other priorities. Tourism is also a key factor and the main concern here is ensuring that, despite the influx of visitors and the threat of fossilization, the area remains essentially a working environment.

The North Pennines cover a wide area. Stretching almost from the Lake District to the city of Durham and from the Eden valley to just south of Hadrian's Wall, the region has something for everyone. Above all, it is a walker's paradise – a land of wild flowers, rare plants and rumpled carpets of purple heather.

The region, which includes 30 Sites of Special Scientific Interest, is also the haunt of Merlins, Grouse and Buzzards. The rivers play their part too – among them the Tees, South Tyne and Wear. Wherever you travel in the North Pennines, there are constant echoes of the region's industrial past. Lead mining was the chief industry here and Weardale's landscapes are littered with its remains. It is also the Land of the Prince Bishops, the powerful and autocratic Bishops of Durham who once ruled this part of the north-east. Further south is Teesdale, renowned for the highest waterfall in England and perhaps more tourist-orientated than other parts of the region.

Anyone exploring the area on foot will discover a host of delights awaiting them. Undertaking a walk in this part of the world is much more than just a stroll in the great outdoors. With the right choice and in good conditions, it is likely to be exhilarating, breathtaking, educational and entertaining. The routes I have chosen for this book largely avoid the high peaks and summits and the vast tracts of open moorland by keeping to clear, less remote paths and tracks on the lower ground, in some cases visiting villages and small towns along the way. The walks are designed to offer a blend of fine scenery and local interest. Many accurately reflect aspects of life in the hills today.

Between 3½ and 10 miles, the walks, all of which are circular, are deliberately intended to appeal to those whose idea of a ramble in the countryside is something reasonably undemanding and, on the whole, quite easy to complete, allowing all day at the most, if walking at a leisurely pace. One or two are more strenuous and are therefore suited to the more adventurous, where a basic knowledge of moorland walking is perhaps desirable. However, anyone who has ever completed the Pennine Way will not find these routes a problem.

The question of footpath erosion continues to crop up. As with popular walks in other parts of the country, some routes in the North Pennines are well used and here there is justifiable concern for their long-term future.

Other paths are lesser-known and in these cases there is a need to promote them in order to keep them open and well maintained. In other words, if we don't use them, we may lose them. Some of the routes I have selected for this book inevitably coincide with those that are already well established. To take advantage of the beauty of the North Pennines, it would be difficult to avoid them. I would also be failing to provide a representative picture of the region if I did not include them. However, many of the walks I have chosen are over little used paths where the scenery is no less spectacular.

Tales and Ales

All the walks begin at a traditional inn where food and real ale are served. Many welcome families too. Most have their own car park unless I have said otherwise and in most cases the landlord has given permission for a car to be parked at the inn whilst you undertake the walk. Many of the pubs are quite historic and some have an interesting and colourful background. Telephone numbers, times of opening and details regarding ales are all listed.

Safety in the hills

A stout pair of walking shoes or boots is essential. In winter, warm trousers, a wind-proof anorak, thick socks, woollen sweater or thermal jacket are recommended – particularly on the longer walks and the hilly, moorland stretches. Whatever the season, whatever the length of the walk, always take a small rucksack containing waterproof clothing. Remember the weather can change swiftly and dramatically in the North Pennines. The higher the ground the more severe the conditions. Take the necessary precautions on the more elevated routes and carry emergency rations – as well as a compass for the moorland stretches.

The very short walks should not pose a problem for anyone – the medium and longer routes are best attempted by those who have some degree of experience. Though route-finding instructions are included for each walk, together with sketch maps, I would urge you to carry a copy of the relevant OS Landranger, Pathfinder or Outdoor Leisure map. The landscape changes constantly and a walking guide cannot be regarded as a permanently accurate record. The distances given for the walks are all approximate.

Public transport

A comprehensive leaflet, 'Across the roof of England', listing times of trains and buses and other general information about public transport in the North Pennines is available from tourist information centres.

A brief summary of the walks.

Route 1. Quite a long walk, though not particularly strenuous, which at one point cuts through the grounds of Featherstone Castle.

Route 2. A fairly short walk briefly exploring stretches of open moorland and visiting the site of a Roman fort near Hadrian's Wall.

Route 3. A walk of medium length, which visits Talkin Tarn and then follows the splendid rock-strewn gorge of the River Gelt.

Route 4. Following the track-bed of a disused railway line and then returning along the South Tyne valley, this is a walk of $5\frac{1}{2}$ miles mainly on level ground.

Route 5. Quite a short walk beginning in Allendale Town and exploring the Allen valley. The surrounding Pennines inspired Catherine Cookson to set her trilogy 'The Mallens' in this area.

Route 6. A varied walk of $4\frac{1}{2}$ miles combining peaceful woodland stretches with open, windswept ground above Hexham.

Route 7. A long walk in the Eden valley, passing fascinating man-made caves set in sandstone cliffs and the site of a ghostly prehistoric stone circle.

Route 8. The spectacular fells of the North Pennines are constantly within sight on this blustery, medium-length walk beginning in the remote village of Melmerby.

Route 9. This walk can be shortened by riding a stretch of it on England's highest narrow gauge railway. The little church at Kirkhaugh is one of the highlights.

Route 10. A walk over Alston Moor illustrates examples of its industrial and agricultural heritage. The return leg of this undemanding $4\frac{1}{4}$ mile circuit is along a stretch of the Pennine Way.

Route 11. The pretty village of Garrigill is the starting point for this walk, which has good views over Alston Moor and visits spectacular Ashgill Force.

Route 12. A lengthy walk, quite strenuous in places, crossing open moorland. Beginning in Allenheads, the route offers a fascinating insight into Weardale's lead-mining past.

Route 13. A short walk around the lovely, unspoilt estate village of Blanchland. The inn here has a fascinating history. A little climbing is involved.

Route 14. A medium-length, windswept walk traversing the slopes and moorland country above the old lead-mining village of Rookhope. There is some climbing by road.

Route 15. Stanhope and its glorious riverside setting in Weardale can often be glimpsed on this 6¼ mile walk.

Route 16. Dufton is on the Pennine Way and this 6 mile route, which involves only gentle climbing, explores the lower slopes of Dufton Pike.

Route 17. A varied walk of 6 miles encountering the Settle – Carlisle Railway and visiting historic Appleby Castle in its closing stages.

Route 18. Brough Castle is one of the major highlights on this scenic walk of 4½ miles.

Route 19. The historic settlement of Kirkby Stephen is midway round this short 3½ mile walk in the Eden valley.

Route 20. The spectacular scenery of Teesdale provides the backdrop to this long walk. High Force, one of the natural wonders of Northern England, is seen on the return leg.

Route 21. Much of Teesdale is viewed on this 6 mile walk which begins in Middleton-in-Teesdale and follows a stretch of the Pennine Way.

Route 22. Cotherstone is the starting point for this fairly short walk along the banks of the Balder.

Route 23. A combination of natural beauty and local history form the basis for this medium-length walk, which begins in Barnard Castle.

Route 24. This is a pretty 6¼ mile walk of pleasant views, fields and woodland to the west of the village of Staindrop.

Route 25. Beginning at Witton-le-Wear, the walk of 6½ miles follows the Wear to the historic Saxon church at Escomb.

1. Haltwhistle

Route: The Spotted Cow, Haltwhistle – Wydon Eals – River South Tyne – Featherstone Castle – South Tyne Trail – Rowfoot – Bellister Castle – The Spotted Cow, Haltwhistle

Distance: 8½ miles

Maps: OS Pathfinder 546 and 549, OS Landranger 86 and 87

Start: The Spotted Cow, Castle Street, Haltwhistle

Public transport: Wright Bros operate service 681 to Alston. Northumbria/Cumberland Motor Services operate service 685 between Newcastle and Carlisle. Trains, running between Carlisle and Newcastle, stop at Haltwhistle.

The Spotted Cow, Haltwhistle (01434 320327)

The Spotted Cow, on the eastern outskirts of Haltwhistle, is a quaint cottagey sort of pub – in fact it was originally built as a row of four cottages. From the outside, with its creeper-covered frontage, it still retains the look and appearance of a private house. Dating back to about 1845, the inn is reputedly haunted.

Inside, there are lots of features, including a wealth of beams. Food is served and the real ales include Courage, Boddingtons, Marston Pedigree, Ruddles Best Bitter and Websters. The Spotted Cow, which is a free house, has a car park and three en suite bedrooms. Look for the sign outside – canny food, canny ale, canny crack! Times of opening are 12.00 – 3.00 and 6.30 – 11.00 between Monday and Saturday and 12.00 – 3.00 and 7.00 – 10.30 on Sunday. The inn is closed Tuesday lunchtime.

Haltwhistle

The pretty name of this bustling little market town somehow conjures up nostalgic images of steam travel. Situated at the confluence of the South Tyne and the Haltwhistle Burn, the town has long been a popular holiday base for visitors touring the area – particularly Hadrian's Wall which is only a mile or so to the north. Coal mining was once Haltwhistle's major industry – these days it concentrates on the manufacture of industrial paints and chemicals. One of the town's most distinctive features is the Old Courthouse, and close by is the Red Lion Hotel which includes a peel-tower. Haltwhistle's townsfolk as well as its animal population would use the tower to shelter from invading cattle thieves.

The Spotted Cow

Featherstone Castle

Although not open to the public, Featherstone Castle can easily be seen from the route of the walk. Splendidly located on the banks of the South Tyne, surrounded by spectacular hills and wooded valleys, the castellated Castle was once a 13th century peel-tower which later became a Jacobean mansion. Its original role was to defend the river crossing.

The house, at one time the home of the de Featherstonehaugh family, is said to be haunted. True or false, it is a classic ghost story with all the right ingredients to form the basis for an historic novel.

The Baron of Featherstonehaugh, disapproving of his daughter's suitor, insisted that she marry a relative instead. But the girl's original lover, inconsolable after she had rejected him, pledged to win her back. With murder in his heart he set off to find her and at the hunting party following the wedding, he confronted those guarding her with bloody consequences. A violent battle ensued, resulting in many fatalities – including the bride. Her lover subsequently took his own life. Meanwhile the Baron was waiting at the Castle for the wedding guests to return, unaware of what had happened. On the stoke of midnight the ghosts of those slain arrived, their luminous faces eerily covered in blood. The Baron apparently crossed himself and the spirits were promptly blown away by a gust of wind. They are said to return to Featherstone Castle annually on the anniversary of the ill-fated wedding.

Featherstone Castle

More recently, during the Second World War, the grounds of the Castle were used as a Prisoner of War camp, with a collection of huts housing up to 7,000 prisoners. The remains of the huts can still be identified today. Very few prisoners ever escaped and, according to local records, most of them had no desire to leave their Castle prison anyway – their matchless parkland surroundings clearly more impressive than anything they had experienced at home! A plaque in the grounds reads:

"Here was the entrance to Prisoner of War camp 18 where thousands of German officers were held in the years 1945-48. The interpreter since January 1946 was Captain Herbert Sulzbach OBE who dedicated himself to making this camp a seed-bed of British – German reconciliation. Our two nations owe him heartfelt thanks. The friends and members of the Featherstone Park association of former inmates of Camp 18. 1982."

The Walk

1. Emerging from the inn turn left and walk along Castle Street. Pass the Grey Bull Hotel, the tourist information centre and rows of shops. On the right is the War Memorial Hospital and park. When the road bends left, just before the New Inn, go straight on, keeping to the left of the pub, to join the main A69.

2. Follow the main road in a westerly direction until you reach a turning on the left for Plenmeller and Alston. Take the turning, which is just before the cemetery, and follow the road as it gradually curves left towards the bridge over the South Tyne. Just before it, bear right opposite some bungalows. Follow the single track lane as it cuts through a landscape of fields and woodland. Pass over the Tipalt Burn close to where it joins the South Tyne. Follow the lane to Wydon — the first of two farms.

3. Pass through several gates and follow the track up the slope to two gates. Avoid the right-hand gate and follow the waymarker arrow. Go through the next gate in the field corner and then make for the bottom right hand corner of the field, where there is a stile. Follow the field edge with light woodland on the left. Look for a gate in the left boundary and follow a path half-right down through the trees. The path descends gradually before reaching another gate. Continue with fence and wall on your left towards the farm buildings of Wydon Eals. Cross a stile and then bear right immediately before the farm.

4. Follow the track all the way to the road at Featherstone Bridge. Don't cross the bridge but instead walk ahead along the road for several yards and then veer left to join a wooded riverside path. Follow it until you reach a footbridge over the South Tyne. Cross the river and then bear right to join a drive running through the grounds of Featherstone Castle, which can be clearly seen over on the left.

5. Pass between some stone gate pillars and note the plaque referring to the POW Camp at Featherstone Park. Follow the drive through the tree-studded parkland with the river a short distance away from you to the right. The drive eventually joins the road. Bear left and walk up the slope between trees and grassy banks. Follow the road as it curves to the right and as it begins to descend, turn sharp left onto the route of the old Haltwhistle to Alston railway. The line, which played a crucial part in the lead mining industry, was opened in the mid-19th century and was in use right up until 1976. Northumberland County Council is adapting stretches of the old line for use as a linear amenity park.

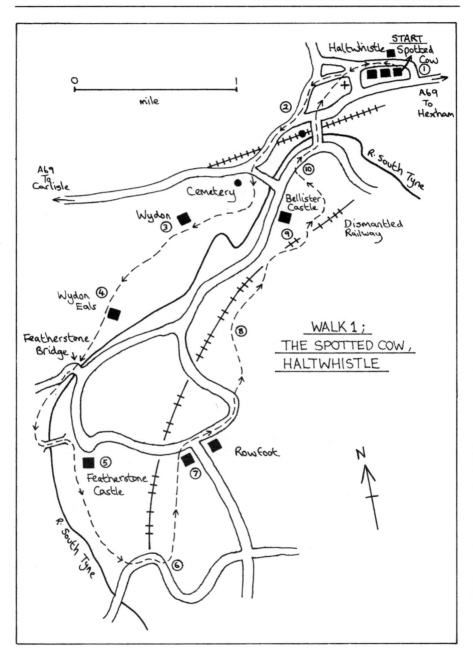

WALK 1;
THE SPOTTED COW,
HALTWHISTLE

6. Walk along the grassy path and here there are reminders of the days when this was a working line. Remains of old platforms and embankments line the route. Follow the South Tyne Trail to the old halt at Rowfoot and turn right at the road.

7. Walk up the lane passing the old Wallace Arms on the right. At the junction bear left and follow the straight stretch of road. After about a third of a mile it bends left under some trees. Beyond the bend look for a ladder stile in the right-hand boundary, just beyond the bridge over Park Burn. Cross the pasture keeping lines of silver birch trees on the left. In the field corner look for a gap in the trees and go up the bank to a gate. Follow a vague grassy path as it sweeps round the field in a broad arc. In the far right corner aim for a gate and then cross over a track to join another track. In the field corner go through a gate and continue on the track. Go up a slope to another gate; the houses of Haltwhistle are visible in the distance at this point. Avoid a track running off half-right and follow the main track down to a ladder stile, then in the next field corner bear right.

8. The route of the old railway comes into view again. Pass through another gate and aim for the trees up ahead. Once through them drop down to a footbridge. Bear left and make for a ladder stile in the corner of the field. Cross into a small enclosure which tapers at the top end. Bear left on joining a track and follow it as it crosses the old line and then swings right.

   At some farm buildings bear right to join a waymarked bridleway. Re-cross the disused railway, pass through a gate and go up the track for about 50 yards, then bear left and go through a gate in the boundary wall. Follow the bridleway as it swings half-right and runs parallel to the old railway line before re-crossing it to a concrete ladder stile.

9. Head up the field to a gate in the next boundary. Aim half-right with very good views across to Haltwhistle. Down below, amid the trees, you can pick out the distinctive facade of Bellister Castle. Dating back to the late 17th century, the castle is reputedly haunted by what is known as the Grey Man of Bellister. Look for the union jack fluttering proudly in the breeze. Walk down the field, ignoring the first stile into the trees and then crossing the next one where there is a waymarker. Drop down into the pretty woodland to a stile and then cross several fields, keeping to the right-hand boundary, until you reach the road.

10. Turn right and follow the road, bearing left when you see the signal
    box at Haltwhistle. Cross the footbridge, built in 1875, over the South
    Tyne, pass under the railway bridge and then bear right on reaching
    the A69. Follow it for about 60 yards and then take the footpath on
    the left. At the church bear left and on reaching the centre of
    Haltwhistle, turn right and return to the inn.

2. Bardon Mill

Route: The Bowes Hotel, Bardon Mill – Thorngrafton – Crindledykes – Vindolanda Roman Fort – Chainley Burn – The Bowes Hotel, Bardon Mill

Distance: 5 miles

Map: OS Pathfinder 546, OS Landranger 86 or 87

Start: The Bowes Hotel is in the centre of Bardon Mill village, which lies immediately to the south of the A69, between Hexham and Haltwhistle.

Public transport: Bus service 685, which runs between Newcastle and Carlisle, stops at Bardon Mill. The village is also on the Newcastle to Carlisle railway, the station is just to the south of the inn.

The Bowes Hotel, Bardon Mill (01434 344237)

The present building, which was built around the turn of the century, replaces an old 17th century coaching inn destroyed by fire. Food is available every day and the real ales include Theakstons Best Bitter and Youngers 70 shilling. The hotel has five bedrooms and outside is a beer garden. There is limited parking opposite. Times of opening are 11.00 – 11.00 in summer and 11.00 – 3.00 and 7.00 – 11.00 in winter. Sunday hours are 12.00 – 3.00 and 7.00 – 10.30.

Bardon Mill

Bardon Mill, once a coal mining community, is now a popular village on the Hadrian's Wall tourist trail. A crucial drove road used to cross the South Tyne here and the local blacksmith fitted cattle with iron shoes before they set off along the route south.

Crindledykes

Crindledykes is one of several lime kilns established in this part of Northumberland in the 19th century. One of its chief functions was to convert local limestone to quicklime for use in farming and building work. Many farmers used it on their land in order to nullify acid pastures. The vast majority of lime kilns had ceased to function by the early part of this century.

Crinkledykes Lime Kiln

Vindolanda Roman Fort

The remains of extensive Roman military and civilian buildings can be seen here in the charming, quintessentially English gardens of a private house. Not surprisingly, Vindolanda is one of many Roman forts in this historic part of the country. The site, which is open to the public, extends to over three acres and the excavated settlement replaced earlier structures of stone and wood. Vindolanda is on the route of Stanegate, an old Roman road and frontier linking various other forts in the area. However, Emperor Hadrian, after visiting Britain in AD 122, ruled that a stronger line of defence was needed to protect these vulnerable and exposed tracts of country, particularly from the unconquered North. The idea of a wall was kindled, stretching the width of the country from Carlisle to Newcastle. Essentially, it was to act as a line of defence against Pictish invaders but it would also help to control the flow of people and trade. Hadrian's Wall, signifying the northern boundary of the Roman Empire, was completed by about AD 138 and ran for 73 miles. It is still regarded as a masterpiece of skill and ingenuity.

The Walk

1. On leaving the Bowes Hotel turn left and walk along the main street of the village. Pass the war memorial and turn left, signposted Thorngrafton. Pass under the A69, go up the lane and then first right towards the village. As the road curves left swing right to enter a field. Aim for the corner of a drystone wall by some trees and then walk along the field boundary with the wall on your right. Pass into the right-hand field and then aim for a stile in the top boundary. Aim half-left to a wall, cross it and over a path and stile into the next field. Bear left, pass through two gates and out to the road at Thorngrafton.

2. Turn left, pass West Cottage, then veer right (signposted Barcombe and Stanegate). Walk up the track; there are stunning views to the south at this point. Cross a stile by a gate, go along the field edge, crossing several boundaries. Begin crossing the open moorland of Thorngrafton Common and after almost 100 yards swing right to join a track running along the moorland edge. As you begin to walk along the track, look for a ladder stile in the right-hand boundary. Aim half-left as you cross this field, cutting between stones to a stile. Just beyond it is a ladder stile. Turn right and follow a track as it curves to the left. Look for a gate in the right-hand boundary wall and go out to the road. Bear left and walk along to the next junction.

3. Turn left here. The road cuts across an open, windswept landscape with glimpses of the remains of Hadrian's Wall on the northerly horizon. Take the next right turning in order to look at Crindledykes. Return to the junction and bear right. Continue along the lane and parallel on the right at this point is the route of Stanegate, the old Roman Road. All that remains of it today is a rough path cutting across the fields. Take the next right turning and walk down to the entrance to Vindolanda.

4. Join the main drive and follow the waymarkers through the trees. The path skirts the grounds of the house, then crosses the delightful Chainley Burn as it cuts through its rocky, tree-shaded gorge. When you reach a footbridge, do not cross it — stay on the same bank. Walk along to a flight of steps leading up to a stile. Cross it to the next stile. Follow the path high above the Chainley Burn. Pass through a gate and continue with the tree-lined burn down on your left. Pass a white cottage, cross a footbridge and on to another gate. Keep the woodland fence on your left. Soon you reach a stile, cross the field to the road, passing under some pylons before you reach it.

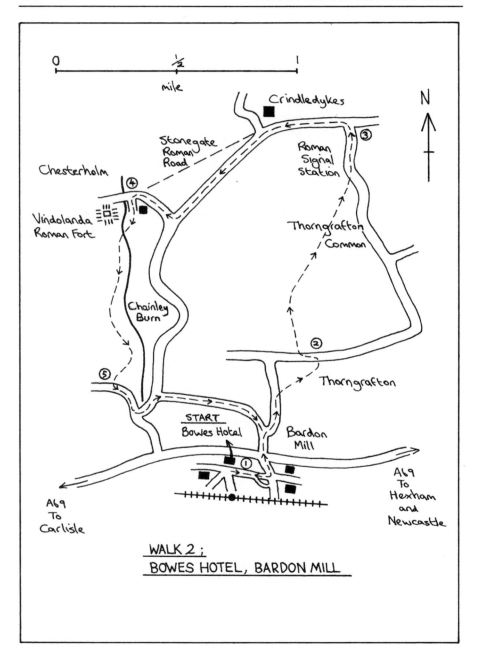

WALK 2 ;
BOWES HOTEL, BARDON MILL

5. Turn left and head for the first junction. Turn left, cross the bridge and then take the first turning on the right to Thorngrafton. Follow it down to the A69, pass under it, then bear right at the junction and return to the centre of Bardon Mill.

The Bowes Hotel

3. Talkin

Route: The Blacksmiths Arms, Talkin – Tarn End Hotel – Talkin Tarn – Unity Farm – River Gelt – Middle Gelt Bridge – The Blacksmiths Arms, Talkin

Distance: 5½ miles

Map: OS Pathfinder 558, OS Landranger 86

Start: The Blacksmiths Arms, Talkin Village, near Brampton

Public transport: Nearby Brampton is served by several bus services; 680, which runs between Alston, Brampton and Carlisle and is operated by Wright Bros, and 685 which is the Newcastle to Carlisle service. Brampton is also on the Newcastle – Carlisle railway line.

The Blacksmiths Arms, Talkin (016977 3452)

The Blacksmiths Arms, in the centre of Talkin village, is a bright and attractive pub. Originally the inn was the local blacksmith's forge – not surprisingly! Reputedly haunted, the inn, which is a free house, has been featured on several television programmes about this part of Cumbria. Bar meals are served every day and there is also a restaurant. Real ales include Theakstons Best Bitter and Boddingtons. Children are welcome and there is also accommodation. The Blacksmiths Arms is open between 11.00 and 3.30 and 6.00 and 11.00 Monday and Saturday. On Sunday the hours of opening are 12.00 – 3.00 and 7.00 – 10.30.

Talkin Tarn

Talkin Tarn is part of a delightful country park owned and administered by the County Council. In its early stages this walk follows the tree-fringed shore where there are good views across the water to the Cumbrian hills beyond. The woodland here comprises many different species of tree – including hazel, larch, birch, beech and Scots Pine. The tarn is fed by underwater springs and is particularly cold in certain parts – even in summer. Among various species of wildlife, you may catch sight of a spotted flycatcher and a cock pheasant. These birds, traditionally bred for shooting, were probably first introduced to this country by the Romans. Various plants and flowers to be seen at Talkin Tarn include wood anemone and wood sorrel, which has distinctive white flowers and clover-like leaves. This pretty flower thrives on the woodland floor, before the beeches come into leaf, their canopy casting a shade on all the plants and flowers growing beneath.

Popular myth suggests that a prophet visited Talkin seeking vengeance for the sins of the villagers. The people of Talkin showed little remorse, however, apart from one elderly woman who offered the prophet hospitality. As he left, he told her to throw her shovel as far as possible away from her door. During the night Talkin was hit by a terrible storm which wreaked havoc in the area. The following morning the old woman discovered the water in her home had not risen above the level of the shovel, though elsewhere there had been serious and extensive flooding. According to this charming legend, the village without morals now lies submerged beneath Talking Tarn.

The Blacksmiths Arms

The River Gelt

'Gelt' is thought to come from the Irish 'geilt' or 'mad', the river having been described so whimsically by Norse immigrants from Ireland. The walk offers superb vistas of the river as it cuts through one of the most spectacular wooded gorges in the North Pennines. The middle stages of the route are a constant delight and gazing around you reveals numerous clues as to the geological history of the area. Cliffs rise more than 100 feet above the river, awesome, towering walls and caves of soft red sandstone reaching up to the sky, creating a curious, magical almost subterranean world of rocks, trees and plants which can be cold and gloomy even on the sunniest day.

Amid the rocky outcrops and trees, high above the river, is the 'Written Rock of Gelt' recalling the stone quarrying work of Roman soldiers who were dispatched to the area to carry out repairs to Hadrian's Wall. The steps leading up the cliff face to the inscription have been virtually worn away by the passage of time.

The Walk

1. From the front of the pub go straight ahead, over the crossroads, passing the Hare and Hounds. The lane cuts between stone houses and cottages. As you leave the village of Talkin, there are glimpses in the distance of Talkin Tarn, the smooth expanse of water nestling amidst fields and trees. Follow the winding lane down between drystone walls, pass a golf course on the left and continue on the road to Tarn End Hotel.

2. Just beyond the hotel look for a wrought-iron kissing gate on the right and head down the grassy slope to the banks of Talkin Tarn. Follow the path alongside the tarn, keeping the water just a few feet away on the right. Soon the broad path runs beneath the overhanging branches of beech trees, providing welcome relief on a hot summer's day. With the leaves and branches of the trees trailing in the water and the gentle lapping of the tarn beside you, this stretch of the walk is one of the most delightful.

3. When you reach the first boat-house bear left and go up the bank to the car park. Take the exit road and follow it down to the junction. Turn right and walk along the B6413 road. Cross the railway line at Brampton Fell and note the old manned signal box. With so much of the railway system now automated, the discovery of a signal box still operated by hand is a rare if pleasant one. Follow the road through a breezy, rolling landscape of trees and fields.

4. About 300 yards beyond the railway crossing bear left signposted Brampton and Gelt Woods. Follow the sunken track and soon it cuts between hedgerows and fields. Pass beside the buildings of Wreay

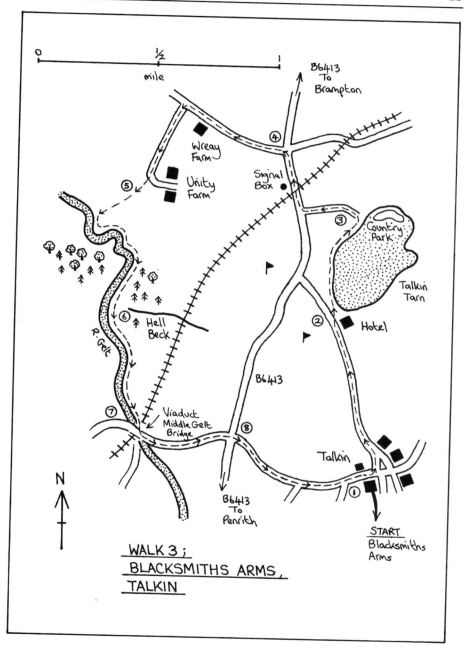

WALK 3;
BLACKSMITHS ARMS,
TALKIN

Farm and continue on the track for several hundred yards until you come to a turning on the left (signposted Gelt Woods). Follow the track alongside a line of beech trees and at this stage of the walk there are good views across to the Pennine chain on the horizon. When the track curves left at Unity Farm, go straight on beside Unity Cottage.

5. Bear right in front of a barn and then swing left after several yards to follow a path alongside a drystone wall. On reaching a stile by some beech trees turn left and then, after about ten yards, bear left again (signposted Middle Gelt).

   Follow the path as it descends into the gorge, between lines of beech trees. On the right, far, far below you, the Gelt – the mad river – dashes through the rock-strewn wooded ravine. The path curves to the right in line with the river, keeping the solid mass of sandstone hard by you on the left. Soon the path bends sharp left and climbs gradually between banks of trees and undergrowth. The Gelt can be glimpsed at times, peeping into view down below in the gorge. Follow the path as it descends steeply via a flight of steps to a bridge at the confluence of the Gelt and Hellbeck.

6. Some sources suggest that the name was inspired by the sight of the water stained red with blood following a battle here in 1570. Continue ahead over the bridge and keep on the woodland path as it begins to climb above the Gelt once more. The playful river is a constant source of delight as it skips and dances between rocks and overhanging trees. This stretch of the Gelt is a favourite haunt of dippers, grey wagtails and goosanders.

7. At length the path reaches the road at Middle Gelt Bridge. Ahead of you at this point, framed by trees, are the great towering arches of the railway viaduct. Completed in 1835 by John McKay, the massive structure, on the Newcastle – Carlisle line, soars to nearly 60 ft. Pass through the arches and follow the road as it begins to climb between rolling farmland. In the distance are glimpses once more of the North Pennines.

8. At the crossroads go straight across and take the road to Talkin. Follow the lane to the next junction and then continue ahead back into the centre of the village. The inn is on the right.

The viaduct at Middle Gelt

4. Knarsdale

Route: The Kirkstyle Inn, Knarsdale – South Tyne Trail – Slaggyford – River South Tyne – Parson Shields – Eals Bridge – The Kirkstyle Inn

Distance: 5½ miles

Map: OS Pathfinder 559, OS Landranger 86 or 87

Start: Knarsdale is just north of Slaggyford, between Alston and Brampton. The inn is just off the A689 (signposted Eals). Coming from the north, turn left at Burnstones Viaduct. The inn is next to the church.

Public transport: Bus services 680 and 681, which are operated by Wright Bros and run between Alston, Carlisle and Haltwhistle, enable you to reach the start of the walk.

The Kirkstyle Inn, Knarsdale (01434 381559)

The Kirkstyle is a simple, unpretentious pub with a welcoming, homely atmosphere. It was built as an inn sometime in the 19th century and extensively refurbished in 1993. It is very much a locals' village pub – though being

The Kirkstyle Inn

close to the route of the Pennine Way, it is also very popular with walkers. The inn provides food every day and there are also three double rooms and a family room. Among the beers are Jennings Cumberland Ale, Boddingtons Bitter and Old Baily Strong Bitter. The Kirkstyle possibly takes its name from the old gate and stile leading into the adjoining churchyard. Times of opening are 11.00 – 11.00 in Summer and 11.00 – 3.00 and 5.30 – 11.00 between November and May. Sunday hours are 12.00 – 3.00 and 7.00 – 10.30.

South Tyne Trail

A lengthy section of this walk follows the route of the South Tyne Trail, currently being developed by Northumberland County Council as a path for walkers. The trail follows the track-bed of the old dismantled Haltwhistle to Alston railway which opened in 1852 and closed in 1976. Evidence of the railway's past litters the route – the graceful design of Burnstones viaduct, with its 6 arches, blends into the spectacular landscape of the South Tyne valley, and at Slaggyford you can see remains of the old station buildings. Being essentially straight and level, the track-beds of disused railways adapt quite easily to recreational trails – or linear parks as they are sometimes known. In the case of the South Tyne Trail, there is the opportunity to admire striking Pennine scenery with the minimum of physical effort.

St Jude's church

The Walk

1. On leaving the inn turn left and immediately pass St Jude's church, built in 1832. Turn left just beyond it and walk up to the junction with the A689. Bear right and walk through the arches of Burnstone Viaduct. Several cottages nestle at the foot of the great structure. The route of the Pennine Way is signposted here. Once through the arches turn right and take the unofficial path up the embankment to join the route of the South Tyne Trail, a permitted path. Access to the trail at this point has been approved by Northumberland County Council.

2. Turn right and follow it south to Slaggyford. The route of the trail is clear and unmistakable, running along the old line between trees and banks of undergrowth, alongside fences, through gates and, at one point, crossing the Knar Burn via the high four-arched viaduct. Running parallel to this route is the Pennine Way. In places it joins forces with the Maiden Way, one of several supply routes to the Roman frontier at Hadrian's Wall.

3. When you reach the old station at Slaggyford, turn left and walk down beside houses and bungalows. Pass the Methodist church and at the junction with the A689, bear right. Follow the road towards Alston and pass Lake House Caravan Park on the left. Swing left on reaching the sign for Barhaugh Hall and after several yards you pass a sign for the Pennine Way. Cross the South Tyne at the road bridge. The river cuts through the deep valley between shingle banks and under steeply rising fells. At this point it also runs alongside the Williamston Nature Reserve, situated on the east bank of the river and in the care of Northumberland Wildlife Trust.

4. Continue along the lane, following it round the left bend. At the next right bend go straight on to join a bridleway leading to Williamston Farm, which dates back to the mid-17th century. Just past the house bear left, go through a gate and then swing half-right to ascend a steep hillside. From here there are far-reaching views across the South Tyne valley. Pass through another gate and continue to a fork. Avoid the right-hand track running up the steep valley slopes and follow the lower, left-hand path with woodland on the left. Keep going and now and again blue bridleway signs are visible on this stretch. Looking across the valley brings the houses of Slaggyford into view now. Negotiate the step stile and gate in a deer fence and enter a

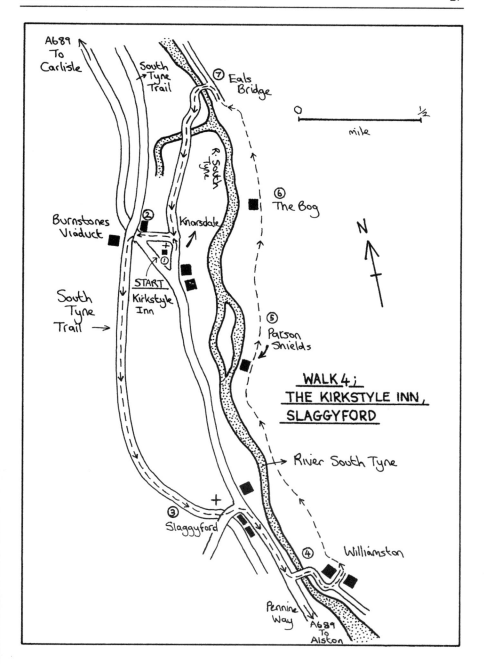

conifer plantation. There is a second gate at the end of it, then immediately a third gate which takes you into a field. Follow the left-hand boundary to a gate in the corner. Descend the hillside towards some trees. A clear track takes you down to the buildings of Parson Shields Farm.

5. Just before the farmyard swing right, through a wooden gate into a field. Walk along the left-hand edge of the field and after several yards begin to veer right to a gate in the boundary. The track begins to climb high above the South Tyne and quickly passes the remains of an old limekiln. Further on, the ground levels out and glancing to your left reveals a fine view of the inn at Knarsdale. Aim for a gate in the far wall. Continue along the track with the dramatic backdrop of the fells behind you.

6. Pass through several gates when you reach a farm known as The Bog, then follow a firm farm lane. Eals Bridge may be glimpsed down in the valley at this stage of the walk. The lane curves to the left and then zig-zags down between trees. Cross Snope Burn and go up the slope. Avoid a turning to Knowe Head and swing left through the trees.

7. At the road junction turn left and cross Eals Bridge – an impressive two-arched stone structure. The river is well stocked with salmon and trout and along this stretch, particularly near Knarsdale, you may catch sight of fishermen standing motionless on the riverbank. Follow the lane with the South Tyne now on your left and later you pass an old wartime Nissen hut. Continue along the lane and return to the inn.

5. Allendale Town

Route: The King's Head, Allendale Town – Scotch Halls – River East Allen – The Kings Head, Allendale Town

Distance: 4 miles

Map: OS Pathfinder 560, OS Landranger 86 or 87

Start: The King's Head is in the market place in Allendale Town, which is at the junction of the B6303 and B6295, south-west of Hexham.

Public transport: Allendale Town is on bus route 688, which is run by Northumbria Motor Services, between Hexham and Allenheads. There is no Sunday service.

The King's Head, Allendale Town (01434 683681)

The King's Head is 17th century and one of the oldest inns in Allendale Town. It has always been a public house. Inside, there is a cosy log fire and a good choice of permanent cask conditioned ales on handpump – including Theakstons Best, Old Peculier and XB, Marston's Pedigree and Old Speckled Hen. There is also live folk music and jazz on some evenings. The King's Head, which is also a hotel, is especially popular with walkers.

Look for the face of George 1st on the pub sign. Times of opening are 11.00 – 11.00 during Summer and 11.00 – 3.00 and 5.30 – 11.00 in Winter. Sunday hours are 12.00 – 3.00 and 7.00 – 10.30.

Allendale Town

Perched 1400 feet above sea level, Allendale Town is more a village than a town. Its compact bustling market place and surrounding streets of solid stone houses have a quaintness and a charm about them. As with so many other communities in the North Pennines, Allendale Town was once an important lead mining centre. Today, the area's economy is based on farming and tourism. Pony trekking, sheepdog trials, golf and skiing are among the local activities and recreations.

According to some sources, the village is the geographical centre of Britain, though this has often been disputed.

Isaac's Well, at the start of the walk, originally supplied the first fresh water to the village in 1849 and is named after Isaac Holden, a local philanthropist whose life is commemorated by an obelisk in the churchyard.

Isaac's Well

Allendale Town has long been associated with various festivals and ancient customs. Perhaps the most famous among these is the curious tar barrel ceremony. Every New Year's Eve the people of Allendale Town parade through the streets carrying blazing barrels of tar above their heads. The climax takes place at midnight when, as the New Year dawns, the barrels are tossed into the flames of a spectacular bonfire in the market place. The tradition is thought to have pagan origins.

The Walk

1. With your back to the pub go forward across the market place and down to the junction by the bank. Cross over to Isaac's Well and take the path beside it, cutting through the housing estate. Go along the side of the green and cross the road to a narrow path between houses. In the field veer slightly right to a stone stile in the right-hand boundary. There are good views at this stage over Allendale Town. Cross the stile and bear half-left towards a line of trees. Cross

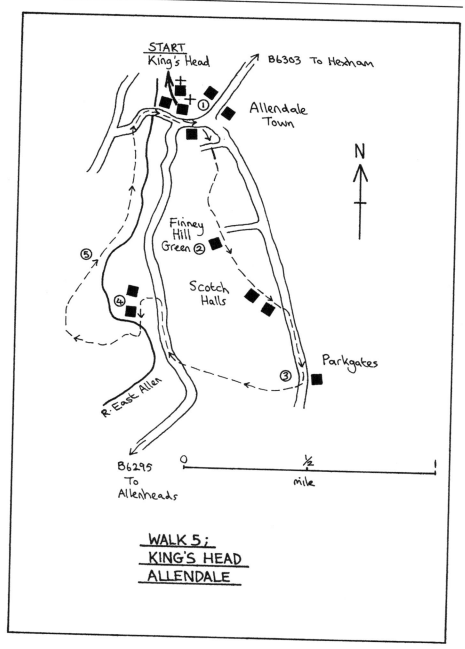

START
King's Head

B6303 To Hexham

Allendale
Town

N

Finney
Hill
Green ②

Scotch
Halls

⑤

④

Parkgates

③

R. East Allen

B6295
To
Allenheads

0   ½ |
                   mile

WALK 5;
KING'S HEAD
ALLENDALE

another stone stile in the top wall and swing right. Make for the opening in the next boundary wall, then the gap in the next. Head for woodland up ahead. Cross a ladder stile and on alongside the right-hand boundary. Go over a stone stile in the field corner and then join a track passing the front of Finney Hill Green.

2. Beyond the farm look for another stone stile and a gate. Cross the field by bearing slightly left. Aim for the ladder stile to the right of the next farm. Cross it and then go diagonally to the next stile by the buildings of High Scotch Hall Farm. Join the farm drive and bear right. Follow it to the road and then turn right. At this point there are glorious views across the North Pennines. Walk down the lane. As it curves left and just before a sharp right bend, look for a narrow woodland path on the right (signposted Studdon Dene).

3. Follow the path through the larch trees and over a delightful little beck. The dark and silent wood is in sharp contrast to the blustery openness of the North Pennines. Follow the path down beside the beck. The route of the path is not always apparent, so keep close to the right-hand edge of the woodland as you descend to the road. On reaching the B6295 turn right and beyond several bends there is a stretch of pavement. Follow the road until you reach the turning to Peck Riding on the left.

4. Pass through the gate and go down the track to the farm buildings. Go through a gate marked 'footpath only' and take the path down to the footbridge of the River East Allen. Cross the river and then bear immediately right through a pretty tree-fringed meadow. Cross another footbridge, then swing left to ascend a flight of steps to a cottage. Keep slightly left at the top and after about 50 yards pass through a field gate. Go straight ahead for about 40 yards and then veer obliquely right. Cross the boundary into the next field. Pass a ladder stile on the left and continue. Make for a ladder stile up ahead, cross a little burn and then you come to a fork. Swing right and cross the turf. Pass through a dilapidated gate in the right-hand corner of the field, then a wooden gate immediately beyond it. Cross the next field diagonally to another ladder stile. Aim half-right down to a gate in the field corner. The houses of Allendale Town are visible now. Cross a stile and follow a clear path with the river glimpsed on your right. The farm buildings at Peck Riding can also be seen on the opposite bank.

5. Keep on the path as it runs high above the river. Cross a stile and then head down alongside the trees. The restful sound of the East Allen is audible at this point. Cross a stile and go across a meadow, curving left with the river still parallel on the right. Cross the next boundary and make for some farm buildings. Aim for a white gate to the right of them. Follow the track to the road and then turn right. It is a short walk back to the market place in Allendale Town.

The King's Head

6. Dipton Mill, near Hexham

Route: Dipton Mill Inn – West Dipton Burn – Black Hill – Hexham Racecourse – Hole House – Dipton Mill Inn

Distance: 4½ miles

Map: OS Pathfinder 547, OS Landranger 87

Start: Dipton Mill is about 2 miles south of Hexham. From the town centre take the B6306. Just beyond the War Memorial Hospital, bear right for Whitley Chapel. The inn is on the right.

Public transport: The walk is not on a bus route but Dipton Mill can be reached on foot from Hexham. The town is on the Newcastle- Carlisle railway. Buses serving the town include 685, 688 869, 888 and 889.

Dipton Mill (01434 606577)

Many inn guides describe Dipton Mill as a gem of a pub. Few would dispute such an accolade. Rural and totally unspoilt, it is reminiscent of how traditional country inns used to be. Dipton Mill has been an inn since the 1800s and originally was part of a farmhouse. Inside, there is a cosy bar with low beamed ceilings and leaded windows. Food is served daily and among the ales on handpump are Hexhamshire Devil's Water, Shire Bitter and Whapweasel Bitter – all from a local brewery. There is also a small family room and a garden where there are barbecues in summer. Times of opening are 12.00 – 2.30 and 6.00 – 11.00 between Monday and Saturday and 12.00 – 3.00 and 7.00 – 10.30 on Sunday.

Hexham

The town, which is the administrative centre for Tynedale, occupies a delightful setting and grew up around the monastery and abbey at a crossing of the Tyne, though twice over the years the bridge over the river here was destroyed by floods. Hexham is a town of great charm and character. Its streets are lined with quaint Georgian buildings and mellow stone houses. A pleasant park with a burn running through it is adjacent to the historic abbey church.

Renowned as a centre for local farmers – sheep and cattle sales take place here at the market – the town is a popular base for visitors to Hadrian's Wall and the North Pennines. Lying in a fertile green valley, Hexham is also home to many commuters who work in the industrial north-east. The nearby racecourse, skirted by the route of this walk, plays host under National Hunt rules and includes several annual steeplechase meetings.

Dipton Wood

The Walk

1. On leaving the inn turn left, cross the road bridge over the Dipton Burn and then bear left almost immediately to join a woodland path. The path is signposted West Dipton Wood. After prolonged periods of rain the ground can be wet and muddy along this stretch. Follow the path through the trees, the burn is just below you on the left. Cross a rustic stile and continue through the woods. At times the path runs hard by the water, then veers away from it between the trees. However, never at any time on this stretch does the path stray far from the Dipton Burn. Keep the water parallel to you on the left and when the trees thin on the right, revealing glimpses of a tree-lined meadow, follow the path alongside the fence. The meadow is on the right. Beech, holly and silver birch are among many different species of trees to be seen here. In the corner of the meadow continue ahead under a thick canopy of beech trees. In autumn the mellow tint of the leaves creates a stunning picture. Further on, the walk runs beside the burn, following a rock-strewn path knotted with tree roots. When, at last, you reach a little footbridge over Dipton Burn, continue on the same bank for about 50 yards and then veer half-right.

2. Follow the bridleway as it zig zags up the bank to become a sunken path cutting between oak and silver birch trees. Gorse bushes can also be seen on the higher ground. Follow the path to the edge of the woodland and aim for a gate. Go straight ahead across the field keeping fence on your left. There are striking views behind you now over Dipton Wood. Further on, over to the right, the buildings of Hexham racecourse edge into view. Pass through several gates and draw level with the grandstand. Beyond another gate head towards some woodland. Join a drive leading to Black Hill, a private house, and follow it beneath some beech trees to the junction.

3. Turn right and walk along the lane. This high ground offers impressive views to the north and south. Pass the entrance to the racecourse on the right and over to the left the buildings of Hexham can just be seen in the distance. If you are undertaking the walk on race days, there is much to see at this stage. Pass a public footpath sign to Dipton Burn and continue to the main junction.

4. Go straight across and pass several houses and a bungalow. Follow the road up the slope between hedgerows. Take the next right-hand footpath (signposted Hole House and Dipton Mill) and in the field

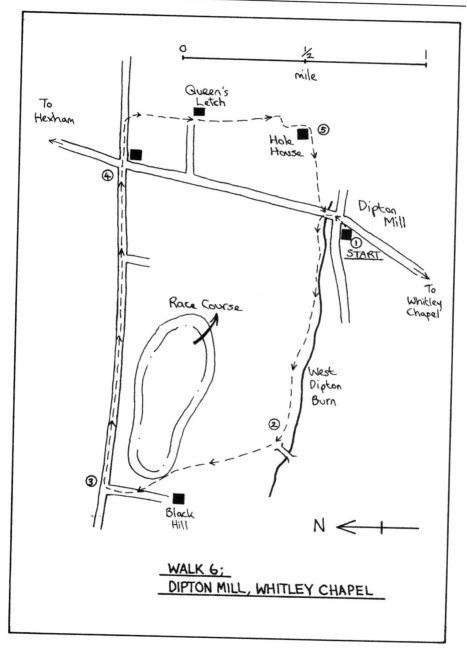

WALK 6;
DIPTON MILL, WHITLEY CHAPEL

corner cross the stile into the next field. There is a sign here —
Newbiggin 1 mile. Turn right, then immediately left — the remains of
an old building can be seen here. Follow the left boundary of the field
heading in a southerly direction towards Hole House. Cross a
dilapidated stile into the next field and make for the next stile.
Continue along the field boundary towards the woodland. Pass
through the gate and into the trees. Soon a house comes into view
ahead. Follow the path alongside stone-built Hole House and after
about 40 yards, turn right at a stile.

5. Follow a grassy ride beside paddocks and cross the next boundary via
   a stile. Look for the gate up ahead in the next boundary and follow
   the track running beside Dipton Burn. At the road turn left, re-cross
   the burn and return to the inn.

The Dipton Mill

7. Kirkoswald

Route: The Crown Inn, Kirkoswald – Eden Bridge – Lacy's Caves – Little Salkeld – Long Meg and her Daughters – Glassonby – Old Parks – The Crown Inn, Kirkoswald

Distance: 8 miles

Map: OS Pathfinder 568 and 577, OS Landranger 86, 90 and 91

Start: The Crown Inn, Kirkoswald. The inn is in the village centre. Kirkoswald can easily be reached from nearby Penrith. Follow the A686 towards Alston and then branch off to join the B6412, which takes you through Lazonby to Kirkoswald.

Public transport: Several local 'Fellrunner' buses from Penrith and other towns in the area call at Kirkoswald about three days a week.

The Crown Inn, Kirkoswald (01768 898435)

The Crown Inn, which is 17th century, is an unpretentious pub with a pleasant atmosphere. It is especially popular with villagers and local characters. Food is served seven days a week and is all home-cooked. Real ales

on handpump include Castle Eden and Tetley. There is no car park but room to leave a car in the village. Times of opening are 11.00 – 3.30 (from 12.00 in winter) and 6.00 – 11.00. On Sunday the hours are 12.00 – 3.00 and 7.00 – 10.30.

Kirkoswald

Peacefully situated in the Eden valley, this is one of Cumbria's prettiest villages, with its pubs, cobbles and sturdy stone houses. The church of St Oswald, from which the village gets its name, has a 19th century tower standing about 200 yards from the main body of the building. In the distance, from the walk, the tower is perhaps more reminiscent of a curious hill-top folly. Kirkoswald also has the remains of an old ruined 13th century castle, which was occupied for 500 years.

Lacy's Caves

The curious man-made caves comprise several ruins and eerie grottoes, which would have been particularly fashionable at the time they were hewn out of the red sandstone cliffs above the river Eden. The Gothic design of the windows lends a heavy air of mystery, almost as if you have accidentally wandered onto the set of a Dracula horror film. Inside, it is very dark but in the gloom I could just make out a series of rooms connected by pointed arches. The caves were excavated by Lt. Colonel Samuel Lacy, who lived at nearby Salkeld Hall during the 18th century. In those days Lacy entertained guests here – a delightfully secluded spot amid the trees. Down below the timeless Eden hurries on its way through the valley.

Long Meg and Her Daughters

Long Meg and her Daughters

Local legend suggests that Long Meg and her Daughters were a coven of witches who were turned to stone by a magician as they celebrated their Sabbath. It is claimed that if you sit at the exact centre of the stones, you can witness the winter sun setting behind Long Meg – a magical sight. This famous landmark is one of the largest Neolithic circles in the country. There are about 68 stones in an oval. The tallest stone, Long Meg, is a 15 foot sandstone pillar and stands just outside the other stones. There is also a suggestion that no-one can count the same number of stones twice. If they do, Long Meg will come to life. Cumbria has a number of prehistoric stone circle sites – many of them thought to have Druid links. Even in high summer you can sense the ghostly atmosphere here.

The Walk

1. Leave the pub, turn right and follow the main road (B6413) towards Lazonby. Just before Eden Bridge join the path signposted Dale Raven. There are two gateways here – take the one furthest from Kirkoswald. Follow the left-hand boundary of the field with the Eden on your right. Aim for a gate, then bear right. There are some hawthorn bushes on the right. After about 150 yards you will see a stream bordered by trees. Follow the path along the bank to a bridge with high stone parapets. Aim for the next field ahead and follow the cart track with a post and barbed wire fence on top of a flood dyke on the left-hand side. Take the track into the next field and continue with the fence on the left. The Eden comes into view on the right. Follow the track alongside the river and when it turns sharp left towards the farm, go forward across the stile and keep on the higher ground above the Eden. Eventually you come to the field corner where a gate takes you out to the road.

2. Turn right and follow the road until just beyond the bridge. Take the signposted path to Lacy's Caves and Little Salkeld. Look also for the old boundary stone between the parishes of Glassonby and Lazonby. Pass through a larch plantation to a sheep net and barbed wire fence. Look for a stile on the edge of the woodland. Head half-right across the field. Follow the path ahead with the Eden visible down to your right. Continue ahead across the fields, keeping the river a short distance away. Look for a stile in the fence just above the riverbank. Cross another field boundary and then follow the path through light

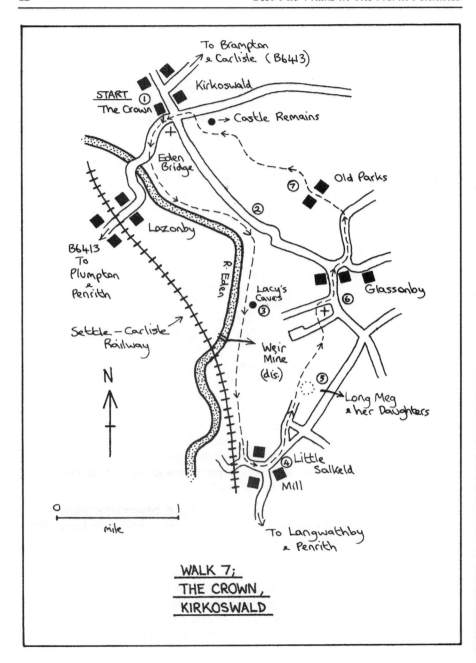

To Brampton
& Carlisle (B6413)

Kirkoswald

START ①
The Crown

→ Castle Remains

Eden
Bridge

Old Parks

⑦

②

Lazonby

B6413
To
Plumpton
&
Penrith

R. Eden

Lacy's
Caves
③

Glassonby

⑥

Settle – Carlisle
Railway

N

Weir
Mine
(dis.)

⑤

Long Meg
& her Daughters

0   1

mile

④ Little
Salkeld

Mill

To Langwathby
& Penrith

WALK 7;
THE CROWN,
KIRKOSWALD

woodland with the Eden on your immediate right. Cross another stile and continue through the trees. Pass alongside carpets of bluebells and cut between lines of yew trees and Norway spruce. The path rises by sandstone cliffs and then drops down to Lacy's Caves. The precipitous path to the caves can be wet and slippery and there are sheer drops – so beware!

3. Continue along the woodland path as it undulates through the trees. Soon a viaduct on the Settle to Carlisle Railway comes into view. This is Long Meg Viaduct cutting across the Eden. Four of its seven piers are always under water. Near here, in 1918, there was a train disaster when the Scottish express crashed into a landslip, killing seven people. Continue on the path and soon you come to some railway sidings. The old branch line here is part of the disused Long Meg mine. Gypsum, a mineral used to make Plaster of Paris, was extracted here until the early 1970s. Turn sharp left by an electricity substation, then bear right at the sign for Little Salkeld. Go up the track beside some red sandstone buildings and follow the lane. There are good views over the Settle to Carlisle Railway. At the next junction turn left and walk into Little Salkeld.

4. At the next junction go straight on up the hill. Just beyond the village sign for Little Salkeld, where there is also a sign for Glassonby, bear left to join a farm lane to the next junction. Go straight ahead along the lane and soon you reach Long Meg and her Daughters. Swing half-right here to join a path for Glassonby.

5. Keep on the path as it runs down several fields, with the hedge line on your right. Make for a gate in the corner. There are now two fields in front of you. Enter the right-hand field and follow its left-hand boundary. In the next corner go through a gate and along the edge of a plantation. At the end of the trees continue ahead along a field edge – the boundary wall on your left. At the road go straight across and head towards Addingham church, built of distinctive red sandstone. Cross the churchyard to the gate in the right-hand corner, then go down the lane to the junction.

6. Turn left and walk down to Glassonby, bearing right at the sign for Alston and Gamblesby. When the road curves right, swing left for Glassonby Beck and Old Parks. Follow the lane between fields, bear left over Hazelrigg Beck and go up the hill. Turn left for Old Parks and take the track up to the farm buildings. Go round to the left and into

the farmyard. With the house on your left, go forward to a pair of farm gates. Take the left-hand gate and keep the fence on the right.

7. Pass through another gate and as the track curves to the left, go straight on to reach another gate. Continue with woodland on your left. As the trees veer away to your left, cross the field diagonally to the bottom corner where there is a gate. Follow the edge of the field with woodland on the left and eventually you reach a gate in the corner. Go straight ahead on a grassy track running up between hillocks. Follow the track to the next boundary where there are two gates. Take the right-hand gate and continue to the next set of gates. The remains of Kirkoswald castle are visible now. Walk ahead with a wooded bluff on the right. Make for the next gate, where there is a good view of the castle, and then join a track running alongside the ruins. At the next gate bear left and follow the road back into Kirkoswald. Turn right at the junction, then right again and back to the centre of the village.

8. Melmerby

Route: Shepherds Inn, Melmerby – Gale Hall – Sunnygill Beck – Row – Ousby – Shepherds Inn, Melmerby

Distance: 5¼ miles

Map: OS Pathfinder 578, OS Landranger 91

Start: Shepherds Inn, Melmerby – on the A686 between Penrith and Alston.

Public transport: Services X88, X89, 886, 888 run at various times between Penrith and Alston.

Shepherds Inn, Melmerby (01768 881217)

An extremely popular and well known pub in the North Pennines, the Shepherds Inn has a fine reputation for food and drink and is renowned for its wide selection of cheeses. The inn is a spacious sandstone building overlooking the village green and the North Pennines beyond. Not surprisingly, there is a strong emphasis on food here. Walkers and children are welcome, and those just wanting lighter bar snacks are well catered for. Among the beers available on handpump are Jennings Cumberland Ale and Sneck Lifter and Marston's Pedigree. There are also two or three guest ales. The pub is open Monday – Saturday between 10.30 – 3.00 and 6.00 – 11.00 and 12.00 – 3.00 and 7.00 – 10.30 on Sunday.

The Fox, Ousby

The Fox inn was most probably built as a farmhouse; parts of it date back to the 17th century. For many years it was known as the Fox and Hounds and it is thought that members of the local hunt met here. It is quite likely that it was run specifically for the huntsmen and did not operate as a conventional village inn until the turn of the century when it became known simply as The Fox. The inn is open between 12.00 – 3.00 and 7.00 – 11.00 between Monday and Saturday and 12.00 – 3.00 and 7.00 – 10.30 on Sunday. The Fox is not open at lunchtime during the summer.

Melmerby

Situated at the foot of Hartside Pass, on the western extremity of the North Pennines, the village of Melmerby has a number of stone houses and cottages surrounding its spacious green. Among them is the old school house with its distinctive clock tower which has become something of a local landmark over the years. The school was closed in the mid-1970s and converted to private houses. Cock fighting and wrestling were once regular activities on the green. The Maidens Way runs across the hills here, a Roman Road leading ultimately to Hadrian's Wall.

The old school, Melmerby

The Village Bakery, Melmerby

Just across the road from the inn is the famous award-winning Village Bakery which has been using wholemeal flour from a nearby watermill since the mid-1970s. Originally an old pig sty and chicken loft before being converted into a smart new bakery and restaurant, its owners have gained an enviable reputation for promoting healthy food and using ingredients produced by organic means. In 1991 a new wood-fired brick oven was installed, the adjoining greenhouse trapping the heat from it, which in turn helps to generate a healthy environment for propagating plants. Try, as I did, one of their savoury snacks or cakes which you could take with you on the walk for added sustenance.

The Walk

1. On leaving the inn bear left and walk away from the main A686 towards Ousby. Pass various houses and cottages and when the road bends right, walk straight on towards Melmerby Fell. There are cottages and farm buildings on the left. Head up the slope between drystone walls and soon the village is far behind as you enter a remote world of smooth, rounded hills and afforested slopes — Pennine country.

The Shepherds Inn

2. Take the track on the right towards Gale Hall. The Pennine views are magnificent as you follow the track over a cattle grid and on to the farm. Cut between the buildings and turn right just beyond the main house. Pass through a gate and then follow the track out across the fields.

3. Drop down the slope and as you approach the corner of the field, veer away from the track and, with trees hard by you on the left, go down to a gateway where there is a yellow waymarker. Cross the field to a stile on the far side; in the next field follow the right-hand boundary.

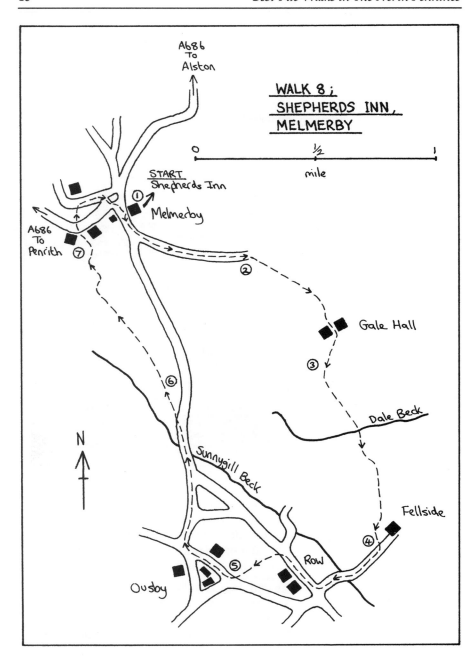

A686
To
Alston

WALK 8 ;
SHEPHERDS INN,
MELMERBY

0   ½   1
                         mile

START
Shepherds Inn
① Melmerby
②
Gale Hall
③
Dale Beck
A686
To
Penrith ⑦
⑥
Sunnygill Beck
N
↑
Fellside
④
Row
⑤
Ousby

On the far side of the field aim for a footbridge over the Dale Beck. Cross a stile and then follow a path alongside a drystone wall. Pass a corrugated hay barn and walk ahead across a pasture enclosed by trees and steep banks. Pass through a gate and then, after about 120 yards, over a stile on the right. Continue to maintain the same direction keeping the fence on your left now. Go up the slope to a stile in the field corner. Turn right, down to a gate and then on to reach a single-track lane. Fellside, a farm, is away to the left, the hills rising impressively above it.

4. Bear right and follow the lane towards the hamlet of Row. Pass Holly House on the left; sheep and spring lambs can often be seen on this stretch of the walk. Cross the Sunnygill Beck as it tumbles pleasantly through the Cumbrian countryside. At the next junction turn right and follow the lane. There is a stunning view of the Pennine hills over to the right at this point. Pass Rydal House and just beyond a track on the right, swing left through a gap stile and head for Ousby. Cross into the next field via a kissing gate and continue in the same direction with the hedge on your left. Cross the next field boundary and then go forward to the next boundary hedge and out to the road beyond another gate.

5. Keep right at the junction and pass an assortment of houses and bungalows. At the next junction bear right signposted Melmerby. Pass The Fox on the right and then turn right for Alston and Melmerby. The view now is of dramatic Pennine summits. Follow the lane and re-cross the Sunnygill Beck. Pass a path to Gale Hall and Melmerby Fell. The road undulates between hedgerows and trees. On the higher ground look for a stile in the left-hand boundary.

6. Cross into the field and then aim half-right across the grass to a gate and a gap stile in the next boundary. In the next field head for a wide gap between two belts of woodland — the distinctive and unmistakable hues of larch trees adding an extra dash of colour to the scene. Make for a gate nearest to the left-hand burst of woodland and join a track running along the right-hand edge of the trees. The houses of Melmerby come into view now. Pass a cottage and some farm buildings and go through another gate. As you approach the next collection of buildings turn right by some trees and go down to a stile and a flight of steps leading to the main A686.

7. Turn right towards Melmerby and after about 60 yards look for a red

door in the wall on the opposite side of the road. Enter thick pine woodland and follow the clear path through the trees. Even on a sunny day it is very dark and gloomy in the woodland — reminiscent of a scene from a children's fairytale. At the end of the wood go through another gate, turn right and walk along to the village green at Melmerby. The inn is across the main road.

9. Alston

Route: The Angel, Alston – South Tynedale Railway – River South Tyne – Randalholme – The Angel, Alston

Distance: 5¼ miles

Map: OS Pathfinder 569, OS Landranger 86 or 87

Start: The Angel is in Front Street, Alston, on the hill just below the market square.

Public transport: Many bus services call at Alston – including X88, X89, 101, 680, 681, 886, 888 and 889.

The Angel, Alston (01434 381363)

The Angel is a 17th century stone-built coaching inn and, like so many buildings in Alston, is perched on the side of a steep hill. For a time it was the Town Hall and the cellar became a makeshift prison for defendants awaiting trail at the courthouse. The black-beamed bar is cosy and at the back is a small beer garden. Food is served every day except Tuesday evening. Among the ales on handpump are Flowers IPA and Tetley Bitter. There is a double room, a twin and a single. You can park at the inn or in Alston, where there is usually plenty of room. Times of opening are 11.00 – 4.30 and 7.00 – 11.00 between Monday and Saturday and 12.00 – 3.00 and 7.00 – 10.30 on Sunday.

South Tynedale Railway

The Alston branch line of the Newcastle – Carlisle railway served the isolated valley communities of the South Tyne for almost 125 years, acting as a vital lifeline for those without their own means of transport. The line had been under threat of closure even before the Beeching era, but had withstood proposals to axe it. However, a new road and subsequent bus service finally killed it off. British Rail closed the line in May 1976.

Fighting for its survival had been various groups of railway enthusiasts who later formed The South Tynedale Railway Preservation Society in a bid to restore the line for public use. Their efforts finally paid off, bringing trains back to Alston at last. Following a favourable inspection by the Department of Transport, passenger services began in July 1983, with the first steam engine entering regular service in 1987. The engine was officially named 'Thomas Edmondson' after the man who invented the ticket system used by British railways for more than 150 years.

Trains are hauled by preserved steam and diesel engines along England's highest narrow-gauge railway. You can take the train, alight at one of the halts and then continue on the path beside the track, or begin the circuit in Alston and follow the path alongside the line, admiring the spectacular views across the valley. Work is currently in progress to extend the line further north towards Slaggyford. Trains operate during the spring, summer and autumn and the journey begins at Alston's Victorian station, 875 feet above sea level and located in a pretty setting beside the South Tyne.

Alston Railway Station

Kirkhaugh Church

The little church nestles peacefully amid the trees and fields of the South Tyne. The scene here will have changed little since the present church was built in 1868-69. Records inside indicate that there has been a place of worship on this site for eight centuries. One of its rectors lived to a great age and, with his thick, full beard and shovel hat, was a familiar figure during his retirement. Incredibly, he didn't marry until he was 94! A few days after his wedding he ordered his grave to be dug to save time and trouble should he die in winter.

The church's distinctive and unusually slender spire was the inspiration of Octavius James, a clergyman. It is said he had been on holiday in the Black Forest and was so taken with the design and style of churches there that he resolved to build one on similar lines at Kirkhaugh. This he did without the help of an architect. The plan seemed to work and even today the spire, which Pevsner described as 'an absurdly thin needle-spire,' is regarded as a useful landmark. Its spectacular setting in the valley has an Alpine air about it. Inside, there are no pews – allowing the building to speak for itself.

The Angel Inn

The Walk

1. On leaving the inn bear right and walk down Front Street to the junction. Turn right and follow the A686 towards Hexham. The entrance to Alston station is on the left. The station building houses the local tourist information centre. Cross the line and then swing right for the northern end of the car park, passing some silver birch trees and various picnic tables and benches. Beyond them, as you join the path alongside the railway track, there is a glorious view of the South Tyne. The river quickly disappears from view as you follow the path hard by the railway track. There are thick banks of undergrowth on the left. Distant fells may be glimpsed between the trees and bushes. Pass an engine shed and then at the crossing, switch to the right-hand side of the track. Soon there is a striking view of the river where the railway and adjoining path cross it. On the right lovely wooded fells rise up to meet the distant horizon. Down below, the river is visible between the trees; the soft, soothing trickle of the water just audible on the breeze.

   Further on is Gilderdale Halt and beyond it a sign — 'this footpath is situated on private land and is not a public right of way.'

2. Follow the grassy path, pass under some power cables and continue high above the rushing, tree-shaded Gilderdale Burn, the county boundary between Cumbria and Northumberland. On the right you can see the church spire at Kirkhaugh. Another beck, the Whitley Burn, cascades down through the foliage fringing the path. Pass under some more power lines. The little church is now level with you over to the right. Soon a stile comes into view on the right. Cross it into the field and then veer a little to the right and drop down the grassy slope towards a line of trees and a river footbridge beyond them.

3. Cross the bridge — the river is particularly spectacular here, wide and serene as it snakes between spacious shingle banks under high green fells. Follow the path round to the left and then right to reach a gate. Join a narrow lane and follow it to the church at Kirkhaugh. There is a drystone wall on the left. In a while the lane runs close by the river. Cross a cattle-grid and continue beside the swiftly flowing water. On the left is a steep, wooded bank and on the right is the entrance to Randalholme.

4. Follow the lane as it begins a gradual ascent and then enters some

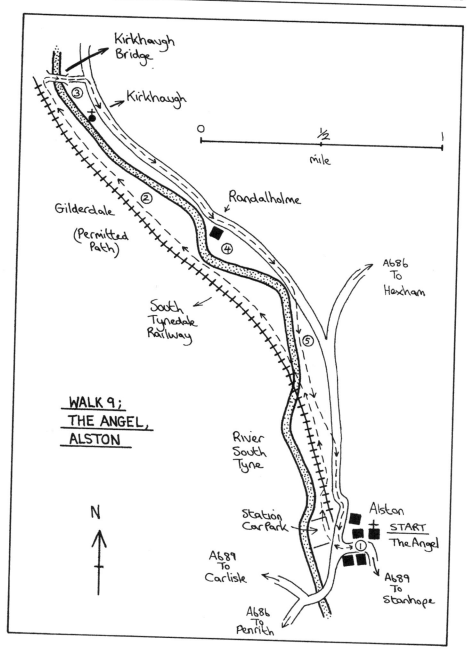

Kirkhaugh Bridge

Kirkhaugh

③

② Gilderdale (Permitted Path)

Randalholme

④

South Tynedale Railway

A686 To Hexham

⑤

WALK 9;
THE ANGEL,
ALSTON

River South Tyne

N

Station Car Park

Alston

START
The Angel

①

A686 To Penrith

A689 To Carlisle

A689 To Stanhope

conifer plantations. Take a public footpath on the right (signposted Alston) and follow it as it descends steeply between the trees. The path is stepped. At the foot of the bank go over a drystone wall, cross the field, or haugh, which means ground surrounded by water, keeping the wall on your right. The river is just beyond the wall.

5. Cross several fields. Then, with the South Tynedale Railway on your right, go forward through a gate in the next boundary and on towards a cottage. Pass through another gate and follow the track to the road. Turn right and go down the main A686 into Alston. Pass the entrance to the station and continue along to Front Street where the walk began.

10. Alston, The Turks Head

Route: The Turks Head, Alston – Fairhill – Annat Walls – Bleagate – Pennine Way – The Turks Head, Alston

Distance: 4¼ miles

Map: OS Outdoor Leisure Map 31 (Teesdale), OS Landranger 86 or 87

Start: The Turks Head, Alston. The inn is in the corner of the market square.

Public transport: Alston is on the route of many bus services – including X88, X89, 101, 680, 681, 886, 888 and 889. You can easily reach the start of the walk by bus from towns such as Bishop Auckland, Stanhope, Hexham, Penrith and Haltwhistle.

The Turks Head, Alston (01434 381148)

The origins of the Turks Head go back as far as 1679. The pub sign illustrates the traditional seafaring mast-head knot. There is a suggestion that the inn was used by sailors travelling between the east and west coasts of Northern England, looking for work and using the old drovers' tracks. This could explain its nautical link. There is another clue inside. It seems some of the inn's beams in the bar were originally timbers used in ship building. The Turks Head has always been a pub. Home-cooked food is served every day except Wednesday. Real ales include Whitbread Trophy and Boddingtons. You can park at the front of the inn.

Times of opening are – 11.00 – 4.00 and 6.30 – 11.00 from Monday to Saturday and 12.00 – 3.00 and 7.00 – 10.30 on Sunday.

Alston

Alston is one of a small number of towns in the North Pennines. Remotely situated at the confluence of the River South Tyne and the River Nent, Alston, perched 1,000 feet above sea level, is often described as the highest market town in England, though that is now disputed as there is no longer a market. With its quaint inns and craft shops, steep streets and cobbled market square, Alston has long been a popular base for touring and exploring the region. It is almost 20 miles or more by road across some of the bleakest and most inhospitable terrain in Britain to the nearest town of any size. Those visiting Alston for the first time are often surprised at just how isolated it is. But from whatever direction you approach the town, Alston's spectacular setting, cradled by hills and high moorland, never fails to impress.

Though the town is small, it is the natural hub of local life. In winter, when Alston can be cut off for days by drifting snow, there is a strong community spirit here, the townsfolk joining forces to battle against the elements.

Alston Moor

Three famous rivers – the Tyne, Wear and Tees – rise on Alston Moor, which lies just above the town. From this rugged landscape, the roof of England, the rivers thread their way through magnificent Pennine country to meet the North Sea.

During their occupation of Britain, the Romans exploited the rich seams of lead on the moor. Mining continued here over the years and by the 19th century Alston Moor led the world as the largest producer of lead. Many of the miners were employed by the London Lead Company based at nearby Nenthead. Evidence of Alston Moor's industrial and agricultural past is seen on the route of the walk.

The South Tyne at Alston

The Walk

1. From the Turks Head turn left and walk up Alston's steep main street. Pass the Post Office on the left and Barclay's Bank on the right. At the top of the street you reach the 19th century Methodist chapel. John Wesley visited Alston in 1748 and preached at the Market Cross. Swing right just beyond the chapel and almost opposite the junction with the A689. Take the walled path and follow it towards Nattrass Gill. The path heads south between fields and pastures. Soon you pass Fairhill Cottages, at one time the Alston almshouses. Follow the lane as it bends left, then right and continues south to reach Fairhill Farm.

2. Pass the farm and glancing around offers wide views across Alston Moor and down to the South Tyne valley near Alston. To the south lie the high tops of the Pennines and Teesdale with the Eden Valley beyond. Along this stretch look out for harebells, sorrel and ragwort growing in the verges. On the left beside the track are the remains of an old quarry which yielded stones for Alston primary school and hospital. The track runs on to Annat Walls, which once consisted of several houses. The remaining buildings date back to the 18th century. Beyond Annat Walls the path runs beside fencing and walls to cross several fields. Over to the west you can see the A686 in the distance, running across the fells towards Penrith. Continue alongside the wall and soon you reach the waterfall at Nattrass Gill.

3. This is a pleasant spot — a favourite haunt of Victorians out for a picnic and a stroll in the countryside. Many different species of plants and wild flowers grow in abundance in these delightful surroundings. The path continues straight ahead across two fields. Grouse, lark and pheasant are among the birds you may spot on this stretch of the walk. Join the farm lane to High Nest, turn left and then right at the junction. Follow the lane down beside several houses including Woodstock and Scarberry Hill. Beyond the curtain of trees lies the South Tyne — at the point where it meets the Black Burn. Zinc was mined in this area until the 1940s. Continue down the lane to reach the farm buildings at Bleagate. Cross Fell stands out clearly to the south now. In Saxon times, some called it Fiends Fell because it was thought to be possessed by evil spirits.

4. Pass through the farmyard at Bleagate and join the route of the Pennine Way. Follow the well-trodden path through countless fields and across numerous pastures, the South Tyne down below you on the left.

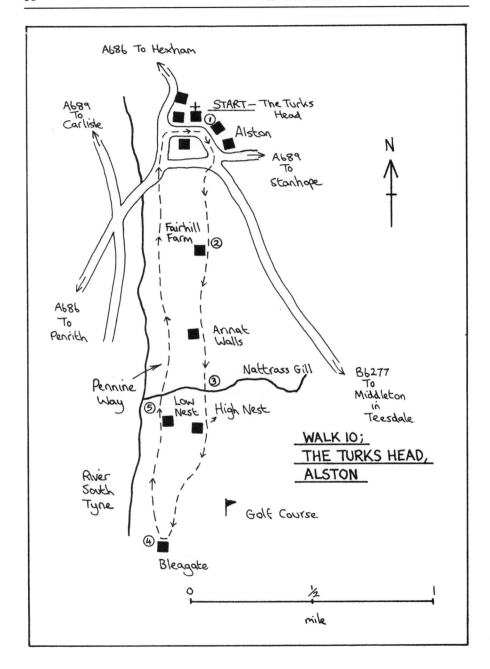

A686 To Hexham

A689 To Carlisle

START — The Turks Head

Alston

A689 To Stanhope

N

A686 To Penrith

Fairhill Farm ①②

Annat Walls

Nattrass Gill

Pennine Way

③

⑤ Low Nest → High Nest

B6277 To Middleton in Teesdale

WALK 10;
THE TURKS HEAD,
ALSTON

River South Tyne

Golf Course

④

Bleagate

0 — ½ — 1

mile

5. Pass the buildings of Low Nest and re-cross the Nattrass Gill via a footbridge. Along this stretch of the walk there are fine views to the west – Grey Nag and Park Fell stand out on the dramatic horizon. After some time the route enters a patch of woodland. This is known as the 'Firs Walk' and is popular with locals and visitors alike. Emerge from the trees and join a road near Alston's cottage hospital. Walk along the A686 until you reach the turning to Middleton-in-Teesdale (B6277) on the right. Follow the cobbled street up to the market square and return to the inn.

The Turks Head

11. Garrigill

Route: The George and Dragon Inn, Garrigill – Pasture Houses – Ashgill Force – Windshaw Bridge – The George and Dragon Inn, Garrigill

Distance: 3½ miles

Map: OS Outdoor Leisure Map 31 (Teesdale), OS Landranger 86 or 87

Start: The George and Dragon Inn, Garrigill. The village is about 4 miles south of Alston, just off the B6277 Middleton-in-Teesdale road.

Public transport: Wright Bros operate a post bus service (No. 889) between Alston and Garrigill. Monday – Friday only.

The George and Dragon, Garrigill (01434 381293)

This popular 17th century inn is a favourite watering hole on the Pennine Way and the first pub hikers reach after the long, arduous haul across the fells from Dufton. Inside, there is a flagstoned bar, a cosy log fire in winter and various artefacts and old black and white photographs – including one of the village school, dated 1931. Food is available every day and among the ales on handpump are Theakstons Best Bitter and XB. The George and Dragon also offers accommodation – there are two double and two single rooms as well as a bunkhouse. There is nowhere to park at the inn, so use the village. Times of opening are 11.30 – 3.30 and 6.00 – 11.00 between Monday and Saturday and 12.00 – 3.00 and 7.00 – 10.30 on Sunday.

Garrigill

Garrigill, once a lead mining centre, is a charming village of stone cottages gathered round a pretty, tree-lined green. The name means the glen of Gerard – a Saxon chief who reputedly led his followers over the tops from the Eden valley in order to graze their flocks in summer. The late 18th and early 19th centuries witnessed Garrigill's greatest period of prosperity. By 1831 the population of the village was over 1500. However, imported lead sounded the death knell on this local industry, many mines were forced to close and by the beginning of the 1970s there were only 135 residents registered on the electoral roll.

Alston Moor

River South Tyne

Between Ashgill and Garrigill the South Tyne cuts through a narrow gorge where the atmosphere is permanently cold and dank. In winter great shards of ice hang from the timeless walls of the gorge and in places the dark river swirls through the chasm and the soft shale like some subterranean stream. It is a curious, entrancing picture. Look out for Rowan, sycamore and hazel growing in profusion along the riverbank. Many different species of flowering plants are known to grow here and the river is also a favourite spot with dippers, herons and mallards.

The Walk

1. Emerging from the George and Dragon in the centre of Garrigill, turn right and walk along the road to a sharp left bend at the Tyne bridge. Continue ahead at this point and follow the path up a steep bank. At the top turn right (signposted Pasture Houses) and cross the field to the next boundary. Pass an old ruined building on the left and then go through another gap stile. Aim diagonally right, down the slope towards some farm buildings. Make to the left of them and pass

through a wicket gate into the old farmyard at Snappergill. The little gate in the wall enabled women and children to fetch water from the stream. Bear left and follow the track to the road at Pasture Houses.

The George and Dragon

2. Cross the road and walk ahead into the field (signposted Ashgillside and Ashgill). This stretch of the walk provides glorious views of Alston Moor. Go through the next gap stile, follow the clear path over the beck and half-right down into the dale. Look for the waymarker post in the next boundary — just beyond a circular depression in the ground. Make for the gap stile and the farm buildings at Ashgillside. Cross into the farmyard, between the buildings and over several stiles to a track. Cross it to a paddock and make for the next gap stile. Turn right and then left, on entering the next field. Follow the path down the slope towards the bridge.

3. Take the signposted path on the left to Ashgill Force. Ash trees in this area account for how the name originated. Soon the waterfall comes into view — a glorious sight as the water races down through the rocky, tree-shaded gorge, framed by the splendid outline of the lofty, stone-built bridge carrying the Alston to Middleton-in-Teesdale road.

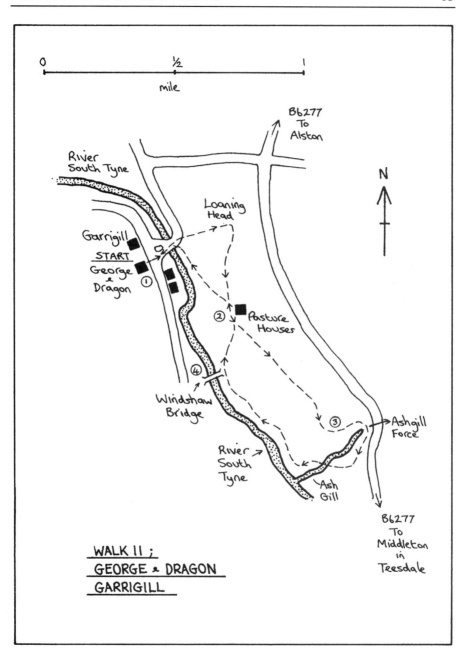

0   ½   1
mile

B6277
To
Alston

N

River
South Tyne

Loaning
Head

Garrigill

START
George
&
Dragon ①

② Pasture
Houser

④

Windshaw
Bridge

③ →Ashgill
Force

River
South
Tyne

Ash
Gill

B6277
To
Middleton
in
Teesdale

WALK 11 ;
GEORGE & DRAGON
GARRIGILL

The bridge was built in 1920 after a previous structure collapsed. Cross the wooden footbridge and walk up to the waterfall; take care in wet and icy weather – the ground can be very slippery underfoot. According to legend, fairies are supposed to cavort behind the curtain of rushing water. Retrace your steps for a few yards; but instead of crossing the bridge again, take the grassy path along the lower bank, keeping the Ash Gill on your right. The path runs up to Waterfall Cottage, a blacksmith's shop in the 19th century, and here you turn right. At the bottom of the slope you are back at the footbridge encountered a little earlier. Cross it, then bear left. Follow the gill and soon you reach another stile at the point where the river South Tyne cuts through a narrow gorge. Keep on the path for some time beside the river; pass a farm bridge on the left. Continue to a kissing gate, then you reach Windshaw Bridge.

4. Cut through the bracken and pine trees on the right to rise above the Tyne and beyond the top fence take the stile and go across the field. Rejoin the path featured on the outward leg of the walk, retrace your steps to Pasture Houses and on to the yard at Snappergill. Turn left into the field and then veer diagonally right to the far corner. The houses of Garrigill are visible now, strung out along the valley floor. Go through the gap stile, descend some steps and follow the path to a gate. Continue to the road, bear left and return to the centre of Garrigill.

12. Allenheads

Route: The Allenheads Inn – Puddingthorn Moor – Wellhope – Killhope Wheel – Carriers' Way – The Allenheads Inn

Distance: 10 miles

Map: OS Outdoor Leisure 31 (Teesdale), OS Landranger 87

Start: The Allenheads Inn, in the centre of Allenheads, between Cowshill and Allendale Town, on the B6295.

Public transport: Service 688 runs between Hexham and Allenheads from Monday to Saturday. There are no buses on Sunday.

The Allenheads Inn, Allenheads (01434 685200)

The Allenheads Inn is understood to date back to the late 18th century and was built as the family home of Sir Thomas Wentworth, who owned the lead mines in the valley. The present landlord collects memorabilia and the inn is full to the brim with it. There are two bars – one is the Antiques Bar, the other is the Royal Room, which has lots of photographs of royalty and a strong nautical theme, including a ship's wheel. Britain's longest historic car rally from Land's End to John O'Groats makes a stop here. Food is available every day, there is a restaurant, a beer garden and among the ales are Burtons and Tetley. The Allenheads also includes eight en suite bedrooms. Times of opening are 11.00 – 3.00 and 7.00 – 11.00 between Monday and Saturday and 12.00 – 3.00 and 7.00 – 10.30 on Sunday.

Allenheads

In the mid-1980s national newspapers reported that Allenheads, a former lead-mining community, was, sadly, a village in decline. It may have been dying but the attack provoked a storm of protest and soon the community was given new life, thanks to the Allenheads Trust, a registered charity whose aim has been to transform the old buildings and draw visitors to Allenheads and its many attractions. The village, reputed to be the highest in England and surrounded by high moorland in the upper East Allen valley, includes a heritage centre and a restored blacksmith's shop. The Armstrong Engine House contains a mid-19th century hydraulic engine used for pumping and winding in the mine, and to drive the saw mill. The estate village of Allenheads was once home to the most important lead mine in Britain.

Killhope Lead-Mining Centre

Surrounded by dense forest and grouse moors, 1500 feet above sea level in Upper Weardale, the Killhope Lead-Mining Centre offers a fascinating insight into the lives of local lead miners and their families. Durham County Council is responsible for restoring the old lead mine and now the centre's attractions keep visitors occupied for hours. The emphasis is very much on active participation and enjoyment. Killhope's most famous feature – certainly the most photographed – is the giant overshot 33 ft. high water wheel, which powered the crushing machinery. You can visit the 'mine shop' where miners slept four to a bed during their working week. Conditions in these 'shops' were often so terrible that some men preferred to sleep in other buildings.

Park Level Mine, once one of Britain's richest lead mines, is opening to the public in 1995. The site is open daily between April and October and on Sunday only during November.

Killhope Wheel

The Walk

1. From the front door of the inn go out to the road and turn right. Make for the junction with the B6295 and bear right, heading south towards Cowshill and Weardale. Follow the road away from the village, rising above the trees and cutting between vast moorland landscapes. Looking back you can just see one of several reservoirs used to power the Armstrong Engine. Pass a sign for the Allenheads Inn and continue on up the lonely moorland road, following it round several bends. At the summit there are breathtaking views to the south over Weardale and beyond. Pass the county sign for Northumberland and then bear right to cross between wooden fence posts onto the moorland.

2. Swing left to the drystone wall and head west, keeping just inside the boundary. Pass through a gate further on and then continue across Puddingthorn Moor, still maintaining a westerly direction. After several minutes glance back and make sure you are in line with the corner of the wall. Pass numerous becks and gulleys which can easily be crossed. However, some knowledge of moorland walking is an advantage on this stretch. The ground can be spongy and boggy in places. Take care underfoot. Look for a currick over to the south-west and head towards it. Do not go as far as the currick but look for a faint track running south into Weardale about 75 – 100 yards before it. Take the path down to a walled track and here there are magnificent views of the dale and the afforested slopes around Killhope. Follow the walled track down to the road and turn right by an old Methodist chapel built in 1858.

3. Follow the A689 and pass a mileage sign for Alston – 8 miles. Continue for about 200 yards, then bear left through a white gate to join a signposted public footpath. Follow the vague grassy path diagonally across the field. There is an enchanting picture here of the Wellhope Burn meandering between the tree-clad slopes of the moorland. Follow the track round to the left and over the bridge. Soon it curves right and runs up the hill towards the trees. Avoid a track running off to the right towards a house and continue towards the buildings of Wellhope. Before them, by the house, turn right on to a woodland ride. The path here has been officially diverted in recent years. On the far side of the trees pass through a gate and continue along the track. After about 150 yards turn right and head for the protective canopy of Weardale Forest. Just before the track bears

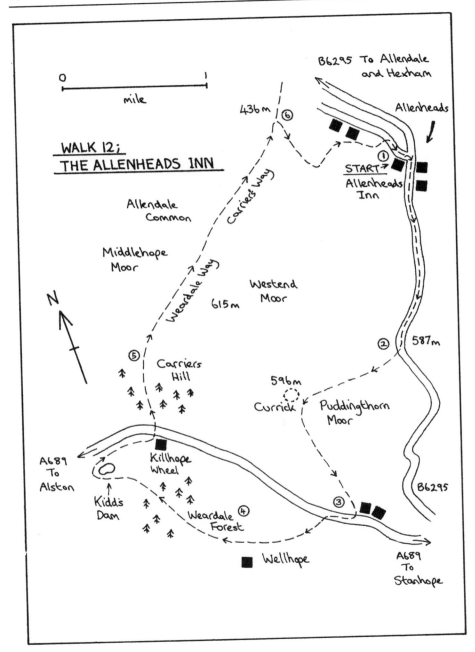

0 ⊢——————————⊣ 1
mile

WALK 12;
THE ALLENHEADS INN

B6295 To Allendale
and Hexham

Allenheads

436m ⑥

START
Allenheads
Inn

Allendale
Common

Carriers Way

Middlehope
Moor

Weardale Way

Westend
Moor

615m

N

587m ②

Carriers
Hill

596m

Currick

Puddingthorn
Moor

Westend Moor

⑤

A689
To
Alston

Killhope
Wheel

Kidd's
Dam

Weardale
Forest

④

③

B6295

Wellhope

A689
To
Stanhope

right at Cowhorse Hush, swing left to the fence corner where there is a stile. Bear right and go up the bank to the fence corner by the trees. Turn right, then left over another stile and into the forest. Incidentally, 'Hush' is a term used in lead-mining, meaning to separate lead from earth by the application of water.

4. Follow the path through Weardale Forest. At times there are glimpses of felled trees and moorland on the left. Keep on the path and pass Kidd's Dam, the dark peaty water reflecting the lines of trees. Just beyond the dam follow the track round to the right and eventually you come down to the entrance to Killhope Lead Mining Centre. After a visit to the centre go out to the main entrance, cross the A689 and join the Weardale Way. The path is also signposted to the Carriers' Way. Cross the stile and follow the wooded track as it curves left immediately. Bear sharp right very quickly and follow the track as it climbs quite steeply. Cross a stone stile and continue between felled trees. The woods here have been acquired from the Forestry Commission and are being restored to natural moorland. Further up, there is an unsurpassed view back across Weardale. The middle stages of the walk as it approaches the Weardale Forest can be spotted from here.

5. At the end of the woodland remains follow a waymarked path ahead across the open moorland. On the summit of the high ground look for a couple of wooden posts. Continue on the clear path through the heather; there are views to the north now, looking towards Allenheads and its reservoirs. Ahead of you is the grassy outline of the Carriers' Way. Drop down and veer right to join it. The Carriers' Way conveyed ponies carrying lead ore from Killhope Wheel to the smelt mills at Allenheads.

6. Eventually you will see a couple of old byres and cottages over to the right on the lower flanks of the moorland. As you draw level with them, join a path running off sharp right and down to the ford. Head up to a ladder stile, follow the field boundary, keeping the wall on the right. Cross into the next field and make for another ladder stile. Cross the next boundary and continue ahead until you reach a track. Follow it as it curves round to the left. Further down, as you approach a gate on the right at a right-angle to the road, begin to veer over to the grassy bank and cross the stile. The route is waymarked. Aim for the right-hand wall of the enclosure and look for a ladder stile in the corner. Follow a clear waymarked path along the edge of the

plantation. Felled trees and deadwood are all that remains of the woodland. Keep the stone wall on the left, pass the buildings of High Shield on the left and then look for a waymarker post down below the bank on the left. Bear left and go down to a track. Turn right for several steps, then left and down to the road. Bear right and pass Allen Lodge. Soon you reach the centre of Allenheads where the walk began.

The Allenheads Inn

13. Blanchland

Route: The Lord Crewe Arms, Blanchland – Baybridge – Pennypie House – Shildon – The Lord Crewe Arms, Blanchland

Distance: 3½ miles

Map: OS Pathfinder 560, OS Landranger 87

Start: The Lord Crewe Arms, Blanchland on the B6306 midway between Stanhope and Hexham. On summer weekends and Bank Holidays the village can become very congested with traffic. On those occasions it is probably easier to use the car park at nearby Baybridge and begin the walk there.

Public transport: Northumbria Motor Services run service 773 between Consett and Townfield, calling at Blanchland and Edmundbyers. OK Travel operate a service (no. 869) between Bishop Auckland and Hexham.

The Lord Crewe Arms (01434 675251)

The Lord Crewe Arms is undoubtedly one of this region's best known and most historic inns. Surrounded by sweeps of scenic moorland, the inn contains many fascinating and charming features. Built in the early part of the 13th century as a guest house for adjacent Blanchland Abbey, the pub, which became an inn and hotel around the mid-1700s, is a solid, sturdy old building – in places its walls are up to eight feet thick. The barrel-vaulted Crypt Bar is a fine example of how the inn was built to last. The Hilyard Room contains a priest hole where Tom Forster of Bamburgh escaped capture. Forster, whose family acquired the inn in 1623, was a Jacobite Commander in the uprising of 1715. He eventually surrendered his Army and was taken to Newgate Gaol. Three days before his trial, Forster's sister Dorothy dressed as a manservant in order to help him escape. Forster invited the governor of the gaol to drinks in his cell, excusing himself after a few minutes. It wasn't long before the governor realised he'd been locked in. Dorothy brought her brother to Blanchland and hid him in the priest hole until she considered it was safe for him to depart to France. The Lord Crewe Arms is reputedly haunted by the ghost of Dorothy, asking anyone she sees to send a message to her brother in France, telling him that the coast is clear and it is safe for him to return to England. Dorothy married Lord Crewe, one of the Prince Bishops of Durham, who bought the estate to help his wife's family after severe financial difficulties overshadowed them.

The Lord Crewe Arms offers food every day and includes Vaux Samson on handpump. Children are welcome and there are 18 bedrooms in the hotel. A pleasant enclosed garden at the rear enables you to relax in peaceful surroundings. From the garden there are good views of the adjoining Abbey. Times of opening are 11.00 – 3.00 and 6.00 – 11.00 Monday to Saturday and 12.00 – 3.00 and 7.00 – 10.30 on Sunday.

The Lord Crewe Arms

Blanchland

Blanchland is one of the most visited villages in this corner of the North of England. It is easy to see why – the place has a timeless quality about it and when all the visitors have gone, it is possible to picture how this tenanted model village might have looked when, in the early part of the 18th century, the trustees of the Crewe estate built the grey stone cottages around the central square to accommodate local lead miners.

White canons of the Augustinian order of Premonstratensians founded an abbey here in 1165. Following the Dissolution of the Monasteries, the monks fled. However, the abbey church continued to fulfil its role as a place of worship. The church was extensively restored in the 19th century. One of

Blanchland's chief attractions is the medieval gate-house which guards the road to Hexham.

Blanchland village

The Walk

1. From the inn turn left and walk down towards the road bridge over the Beldon Burn. Just before the bridge swing right (signposted Baybridge). There now follows a pleasant waterside walk with steeply rising wooded banks on the opposite side of the burn. On the right are pleasant views across the water meadows. Cross a ladder stile and at the road turn right for Baybridge.

2. The Baybridge car park is on the left. As the road to Blanchland bends right, go straight on along a 'no through road'. There are some pretty stone cottages on the right at this point. The lane begins to rise quite steeply and further up, there are wide views to the upper reaches of the Derwent and the unspoilt moorland country above the Beldon Burn. The scene is thickly afforested, creating a stunning mosaic of differing shades and hues. Pass a pine plantation where the soothing

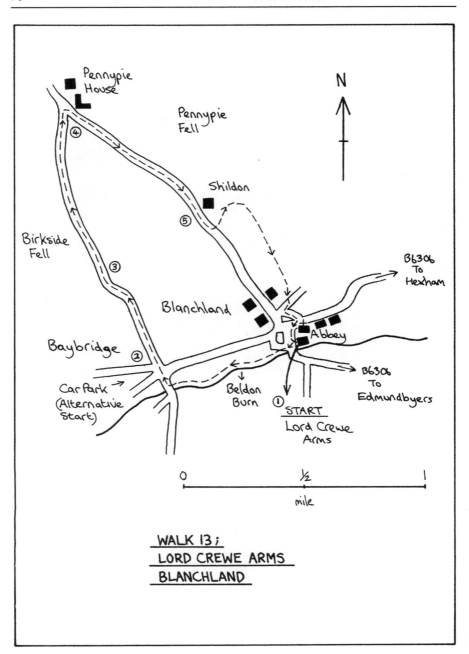

Pennypie House

Pennypie Fell

N

④

Shildon

⑤

Birkside Fell

③

B6306 To Hexham

Blanchland

Baybridge ②

Abbey

B6306 To Edmundbyers

Car Park (Alternative Start)

Beldon Burn

① START
Lord Crewe Arms

0   ½   1
mile

WALK 13;
LORD CREWE ARMS
BLANCHLAND

sound of the breeze in the branches adds to the enjoyment of the walk. Continue climbing and pass a turning to Birkside Farm.

3. Beyond the trees pass through a gate and continue on the 'no through road'. Approach the gate to an installation and veer half-right on a clear track running across glorious heather moorland. The track runs alongside a wall on the right. Cross a stile and continue towards the farm buildings at Pennypie. The track drops down gently through the heather and then round to the right. Pass through a gate and then go straight on down the track. The farm is up on the left. Lapwings may be seen in this area.

4. Follow the track as it descends gradually between the fells. Pass various farm buildings and byres and continue on the main track down between glorious wooded vistas to an old smeltmill chimney on the right. Ignore a footpath to Blanchland Moor and continue for several yards to a path on the left.

5. Follow this path and after about 75 yards you reach Keepers Cottage. Bear right through a gate, then swing immediately left to another gate. Follow the waymarkers and keep the woodland on your right. The path is quite boggy underfoot along this stretch. Beech trees can be seen at intervals. Pass through another gate, go down the bank for several yards to reach a rutted forest track. Turn left and follow it. When the track begins to curve left, take the right-hand fork and on reaching an old dilapidated gate post swing half-right and descend quite steeply on a clear path. Pass a waymarked path on the left and continue down to the houses of Blanchland. Bear left and return to the village centre.

14. *Rookhope*

Route: The Rookhope Inn – Rookhope Nurseries – Lintzgarth Common – Scarsike Head – Smailsburn Common – The Rookhope Inn

Distance: 5¼ miles

Map: OS Pathfinder 570, OS Landranger 87

Start: The Rookhope Inn is in the centre of the village. Rookhope is several miles north of the A689, near Stanhope.

Public transport: Bus number 102, operated by Weardale Motor Services, runs infrequently between Stanhope and Rookhope.

The Rookhope Inn (01388 517215)

The Rookhope Inn offers bed and breakfast accommodation and bar meals. Hikers and locals form the clientele, and John Smiths Bitter is among the beers. There are tables and benches at the front. Times of opening vary but as a rule they are as follows: 11.00 – 3.00 and 7.00 – 11.00 between Monday and Saturday and 12.00 – 3.00 and 7.00 – 10.30 on Sunday. The inn is shut Monday lunchtime.

Rookhope

Surrounded by spectacular high moorland scenery, the village of Rookhope is possibly one of the most isolated communities in the North Pennines. Located in Rookhope Dale, a side valley of Weardale, the village was once an important lead- and ironstone-mining centre in the North Pennine Ore Field. Lines of terraced houses climb the bleak hillsides, built to accommodate the miners and their families. Evidence of mining and smelting can still be seen in the area. Above the village what looks like a stone path climbs up the side of Redburn Common. In reality it is the remains of a two mile long chimney flue designed to draw the poisonous toxic fumes away from the smelt mill and expelling them onto the higher moorland ground. Part of the old flue can still be seen at Lintzgarth Arch.

Above Rookhope are the remains of an old disused railway line running across the fells. The line, opened in 1846 and eventually abandoned in the 1920s, conveyed ironstone and was the highest standard-gauge railway ever built in Britain. Remains of the old railway buildings still survive and a ghostly stillness envelopes these long-forgotten expanses as you picture how this landscape might have looked more than 100 years ago.

Rookhope Dale

Rookhope has harboured a curious and gruesome secret for many years. In 1918 a number of skulls, nine in all, were discovered by a group of workmen in a quarry near Redburn Mine just outside the village. The skulls lay in a shallow grave, eight of them intact, the ninth having been badly smashed. No other human remains were unearthed but in the eye sockets of the skulls a number of bronze coins were found, one of them a cartwheel penny of 1799. It was customary to cover the eyes of the dead with coins, but there is still no logical explanation as to why this site was chosen to bury the dead. The file remains open, decades later, with so many questions unanswered. Most importantly, who were the victims and why did they die?

Rookhope is the home of one of the highest nurseries in Britain. Situated 1100 feet above sea level, high in the Pennine hills, this productive garden and nursery includes some of the hardiest plants to be found anywhere. The varieties are intentionally perennial in order to withstand the severity of the climate here. Alpines, Border Plants, Shrubs, Heathers and Conifers are all produced at Rookhope. A visit to this site is a must for the dedicated horticulturalist. Rookhope Nurseries are open at various times throughout the year.

The Rookhope Inn

The Walk

1. With your back to the front door of the inn, go straight ahead down the road. Pass a public footpath sign on the right and the village hall on the left. Follow the road between lines of cottages and houses. Pass a turning to Burnside Cottages on the left and continue along the road. Soon you reach the entrance to Rookhope Nurseries and Gardens. The Rookhope Burn runs parallel to the road, on the left. Pass a turning on the right to Blanchland and just beyond Lintzgarth Arch turn left towards Westgate.

2. Follow the lane as it bends sharp right by the entrance to Saughtree Farmstead. Keep to the lane as it winds its way across the moorland expanses. Soon you pass a private woodland on the left. Sheep can sometimes be seen nestling amid the pine trees. There is a glorious view at this point down towards Rookhope Dale. Pass a ladder stile

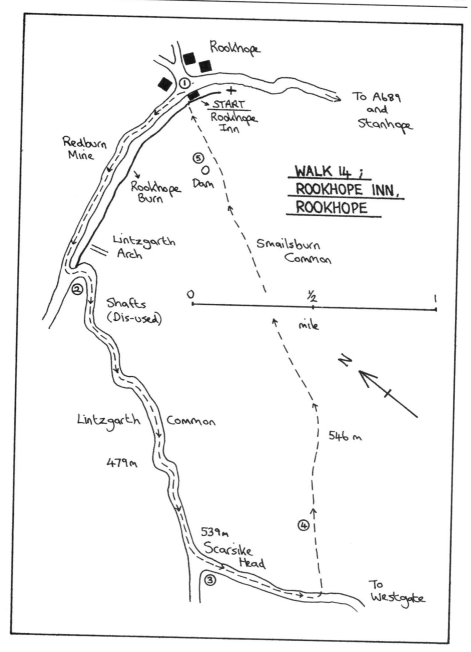

Rookhope

To A689
and
Stanhope

START
Rookhope
Inn

Redburn
Mine

Rookhope
Burn

Dam

WALK 14 ;
ROOKHOPE INN,
ROOKHOPE

Lintzgarth
Arch

Smailsburn
Common

Shafts
(Dis-used)

0   ½   1
           mile

N

Lintzgarth   Common

479m

546 m

539m
Scarsike
Head

To
Westgate

and continue climbing between drystone walls. Eventually you reach the summit and here the surroundings are appropriately wild and windswept as you gaze at a magnificent panorama of Pennine summits and vast sweeps of lonely moorland.

3. Turn left and head towards Westgate. Descend the quiet lane and look for a stony track running off to the left between crumbling walls. Follow the track and in the distance you can make out the cement works down in the Wear valley near Stanhope. Pass between concrete posts to reach the end of the track. Ahead of you is a bare moorland landscape, symbolizing the true bleakness of the Pennines.

4. Beyond the track maintain the same direction across the open ground and at the top of the slope a drystone wall edges into view. Bear right as you approach it and very soon you reach the field corner. There are two gates at this point. Pass through the one on the left and then walk ahead with the wall on your left. Ahead of you are glorious views down to Rookhope Dale. Cross several field boundaries, still with the wall on your left and various houses and farmsteads on the slopes above Rookhope begin to appear. Low-flying jets can sometimes be seen swooping down the dale, moving so swiftly that you hardly have time to spot them. This stretch of the walk coincides with the route of the Wear Valley Way. Pass between some dilapidated gate posts and go down Smailsburn Common to the old lead miners' dam.

5. Keep to the right of it and cross the fence. Continue down the slopes and at the corner of the wall, veer left towards some abandoned cottages and power lines. Bear right just beyond them and follow the path as it descends quite steeply into Rookhope. Cross a ladder stile and then join a track leading into the village. Pass over the Rookhope Burn and the inn is a short distance beyond it on the right.

15. Stanhope

Route: The Queens Head, Stanhope – River Wear – Horsley Head – Hag Bridge – Weardale Way – The Queens Head, Stanhope

Distance: 6 miles

Map: OS Outdoor Leisure 31 (Teesdale), OS Landranger 92

Start: The Queens Head, Front Street, Stanhope. Front Street is the main A689 through Stanhope and the inn is at the eastern end of the town.

Public transport: Bus numbers X21, X88, 101 and 102 stop at Stanhope.

The Queens Head, Stanhope (01388 528160)

The Queens Head is a traditional 19th century town pub with a friendly, bustling atmosphere. Food is served every day, beers on handpump include Theakstons Best and XB and there are four twin bedrooms. The inn doesn't

have its own car park but there is plenty of room to park in the town. Time of opening are 12.00 – 3.00 and 7.00 – 11.00 from Monday to Saturday; on Saturday the hours are 12.00 – 5.00 and 7.00 – 11.00 and on Sunday 12.00 – 3.00 and 7.00 – 10.30.

Stanhope

The town has long been acknowledged as the 'capital' of Weardale. It is a working community with its roots firmly established in local industry – chiefly lead mining. These days, tourism plays a key role in the success of Stanhope's economy. The Durham Dales Centre is worth a visit and includes an information centre, local craft exhibitions and workshops arranged in a delightful courtyard setting. Nearby is a striking gazebo.

The town has a straggling main street of lime trees, shops and pubs, but the focal point is the Market Place, for many years the venue for weekly markets and biannual fairs during the 15th century. Immediately to the north of this spot is the 13th century church of St Thomas and just near the main entrance is the stump of a fossilised tree which dates back 250 million years. The tree was brought to Stanhope from nearby Edmundbyers in 1962. To the south of the church is Stanhope Castle, a late 18th century sham built on the site of an old medieval manor house. The castle was later converted into apartments.

Gazebo at the Durham Dales Centre

The Walk

1. Emerge from the pub, turn right and walk along the A689 as far as another inn, The Bonny Moor Hen. Cross the road and take the lane to the left of the Packhorse Inn, following it down to the banks of the Wear. Pass rows of stone cottages and head for the Riverside Walk. Follow the pretty, tree-lined path upstream and then cross the river at the footbridge. Bear right and follow the track as far as the junction with the road. Stepping stones can be seen here on the right. Continue along the road and when it bends right, take the turning for Horsley Hall.

2. Follow the road and here you can spot the haphazard formations of the Wear's bed-rock down below. The old Heritage Railway Line, which has also been used by Blue Circle Industries, can also be seen. Continue along the lane and looking back, there are good views of Stanhope down in the valley. Pass Aller Gill House and Aller Gill Cottage and continue between drystone walls. There is a gentle ascent now. When the road bends sharp right, go through a gate on the corner and veer slightly right across the field. The trees above Horsley Burn are on the left.

3. Aim for the field corner, pass through the gate and continue with the burn and rushing falls far below you. Cross the next boundary via a gate and there are farm buildings ahead now, just below the horizon. Almost in the field corner you pass over the remains of an old drainage ditch running down into Horsley Burn. Cross the next boundary and then continue straight ahead across the field towards Horsley Head. Tracks appear just before some power lines. Go through the gate and follow the track towards the farmstead just up ahead.

4. Keep the buildings to the right of you, go beyond the barn and then immediately right and up towards a drystone wall running off at an angle in front of you. Keep to the left of it and just before you reach the top boundary, veer over to the left side of the field. Cross a stone stile and ahead of you now is the distinctive Blue Circle cement works chimney — the highest chimney in County Durham. Make for the right-hand corner of the field where a gate takes you out to a stony track. Bear left and follow it until you reach another gate. Beyond it bear immediately right and head down the track beside the remains of an old limestone kiln. As the track curves away to the left, go

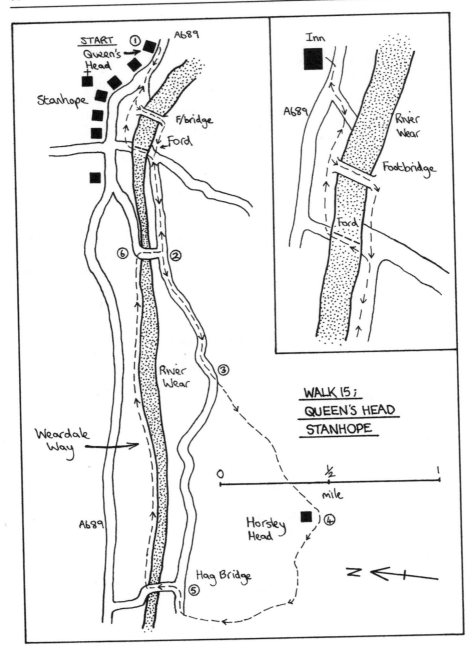

START
Queen's
Head

A689

Stanhope

F/bridge

Ford

Inn

A689

River
Wear

Footbridge

Ford

① ⑥ ② ③

River
Wear

Weardale
Way

A689

WALK 15;
QUEEN'S HEAD
STANHOPE

0   ½   1
         mile

Horsey
Head ④

Hag Bridge ⑤

N

through a gate on the right of it and down the slope. Keep the remains of the old wall on your left. Ahead of you is a splendid view of Weardale. Eastgate can be seen from here and in the foreground the Blue Circle chimney, looking not unlike a rocket about to blast off. Cut off the corner of the field and go diagonally to a gate in the lower boundary. Bear left and go down the field with the wall on your left. Cross the dilapidated boundary wall into a small enclosure. Look for some trees further down the slope and a gate just to the right of them. Drop down the field to the next gate by the buildings of Hag Gate and join the track to the road.

5. Turn right and follow the lane between walls and clumps of cow parsley. Take the first left turning and make for Hag Bridge over the Wear. There is a surprising view of the Blue Circle chimney upstream, framed by trees.

    Bear right to join the route of the Weardale Way – Stanhope is 3 miles. Follow the track to the caravan park and as it swings right, continue ahead with caravans on your right. At the far end of the meadow go through a gate by a toilet block and then bear left on to a firm track. Follow it to the far end of the park, where there is a Weardale Way waymarker. Follow the path with the river on the right and the old Heritage Line on your left. Continue beside gorse bushes, silver birch trees and wild flowers. Come up to a stile and then pass close to the riverbank between birch and larch trees. Pass alongside the garden of a bungalow and then straight on. Keep to the left of the enclosed gorse bushes and follow the field boundary until you come to a concrete ladder stile. Cross the line, then another stile and bear right. Follow the track to the road.

6. Turn right over the Wear, then retrace your steps to the stepping stones encountered near the start of the walk. Cross the river by means of the stones and then swing right and follow the Riverside Walk back to the centre of Stanhope.

16. Dufton

Route: The Stag, Dufton – Pennine Way – St Cuthbert's church – Knock – Great Rundale Beck – Pus Gill – The Stag, Dufton

Distance: 6 miles

Map: OS Outdoor Leisure 31 (Teesdale), OS Landranger 91

Start: The Stag, Dufton. The inn is at the centre of the village, which is several miles north of Appleby-in-Westmorland and is signposted off the A66.

Public transport: A weekly bus service serves Dufton on Friday.

The Stag, Dufton (017683 51608)

The Stag was built around the beginning of the 19th century as an ale-house for local lead miners. Overlooking the elongated, tree-lined village green, from the outside it looks very much like a private house. The name of the inn is associated with an ancient forest used as a hunting ground by William Rufus. In summer it is very pleasant to while away an hour or two by sitting outside in the beer garden, enjoying a pint and taking in the peaceful village surroundings. Cone-shaped Dufton Pike rises majestically behind the inn. The ales at The Stag include Boddingtons Bitter, Castle Eden and Flowers IPA. Food is available every day – though not Monday lunchtime in winter – and the pub also includes two single rooms, one twin and one double. Times of opening are as follows: Winter – Monday – Saturday 11.00 – 3.00 and 6.00 – 11.00 (closed Monday lunchtime), Sunday 12.00 – 3.00 – 7.00 – 10.30 – Summer 11.00 – 11.00 between Monday and Saturday and 12.00 – 10.30 on Sunday. Breakfast is also served by prior booking from 8.00 – 9.30am between April and September.

Dufton

Mention the name of this pleasant, red sandstone village nestling below the summits of Dufton Pike, Great Dun Fell and Cross Fell on the edge of the Vale of Eden and those that have heard of it will probably tell you that its chief claim to fame is as a staging post on the Pennine Way. An atmosphere of peace and tranquillity welcomes the traveller, though some visitors to Dufton, particularly those on foot, are caught out by the notorious Helm Wind which races down from the fells at great speed, often dislodging roof slates and blowing down trees in its path. Dufton Mine was opened during the 18th century; the London Lead Company who owned it did much to improve the living conditions of those miners whose homes were in the village. The name Dufton is Anglo Saxon for 'a farmstead where doves are reared'.

The author below Dufton Pike

St Cuthbert's Church

The present church is late 18th century and replaces an earlier stone building dating back to 1293. Many of the miners who worked in the area are buried in the churchyard, their corpses carried on horseback across the fells. The church is named after St Cuthbert whose body was carried across the North Pennines by monks from Lindisfarne attempting to flee the Vikings in 875 AD.

The Walk

1. From the front of the inn bear left and walk along the road beside the green. Dufton Pike soars skyward immediately behind the village; further away to the north, on the horizon, are the high tops of Cross Fell and Great Dun Fell, with the distinctive white globe of its radar station standing out as a useful directional landmark. Follow the road round the left bend and then as it swings right by Dufton and Knock Methodist church, go straight on to join a track signposted High Scald Fell. Follow the route of the Pennine Way down the slope and after about 120 yards, at the first intersection, veer left through a gate — a sign requests you to keep it closed.

2. Follow the path and soon you pass through two gates in quick succession. Continue between fences and fields and go through several more gates. Cross Eller Beck and go on along the path keeping the water beside you on the left. Pass through another gate, avoid a track running off sharply to the left and begin to approach a bungalow at Coatsike Farm. Just before it take the path heading obliquely left (signposted Knock). In high summer it is quite overgrown here, with banks of undergrowth threatening to engulf the path. However, the route is not impenetrable! Cross a stile, then a beck and follow the path between ancient stones and deadwood. Enter a field via a gate and follow its left-hand edge towards St Cuthbert's church. Pass through the squeeze stile into the churchyard and take the permitted path round the side of the building to a gate in the far boundary.

3. Cross the field, pass over a beck and make for a stile in the next wall. Continue across the next field until you reach a wooden footbridge over a beck. In the next field keep to the right-hand boundary, cross the stone stile and then turn right to follow the lane to Knock. When it bends sharp left in the village, go straight on to join a track (signposted Cross Fell).

4. Follow the track until you reach a stile and footpath sign to Dufton on the right. Keep to the track as it bends left and runs up a slope to another stile in the right-hand fence. Descend to the corner of the field, cross into the field on the left and then follow the path above Knock Gill, a striking wooded ravine. Follow the path down to the water's edge and cross the stepping stones. Pass through the stone stile in the wall and follow the narrow path as it traverses the slopes

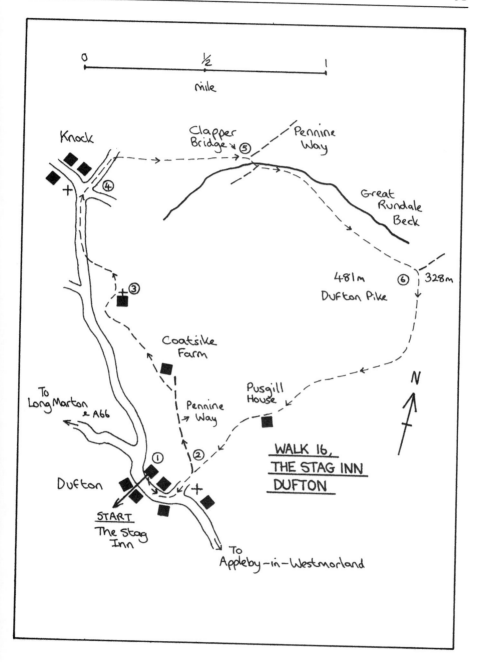

WALK 16,
THE STAG INN
DUFTON

of Great Rundale Beck. Go up to a stile and then head across the open moorland with the tree-lined beck down to your right. Keep going until you reach the next wall where there is a stone stile. Turn right, briefly rejoining the route of the Pennine Way, and cross the ancient clapper bridge over the Great Rundale Beck.

5. Once through the stone stile beyond it, turn left to follow the track along the lower flanks of Dufton Pike. At the next gate go over the adjoining stile. Glancing away to the left reveals a view of the drystone wall running in a neat line up the fellside. Go over a stone stile in the next boundary wall and continue along the open moorland path until it merges with a clear track. The walk crosses an isolated, primitive landscape of limestone shale and bleak fells. Lime was once quarried in this area. At the next junction bear right to join a bridleway running down towards Dufton. A magnificent view of Dufton and the Eden valley opens up before you now.

6. Pass through several gates and continue. The Pus Gill runs parallel to the track. Cross Eller Beck and soon you reach the rejoin the Pennine Way on the approach to Dufton village. Retrace your steps to the road, turn right and walk back to the inn.

The Stag Inn

17. Appleby-in-Westmorland

Route: The Royal Oak, Appleby – Settle – Carlisle Railway – Flakebridge Wood – Clickham Farm – Appleby – Appleby Castle – Jubilee Bridge – The Royal Oak, Appleby.

Distance: 6 miles

Map: OS Outdoor Leisure 31 (Teesdale) OS Landranger 91

Start: The Royal Oak, Bongate, Appleby. The inn is just to the east of Appleby Castle, on the B6542.

Public Transport: Appleby is served by trains on the Leeds/Bradford – Settle – Kirkby Stephen – Carlisle line – better known as the 'Settle – Carlisle' line. Bus services 495 and 560 stop at Appleby.

The Royal Oak, Appleby (017683 51463)

Parts of the building date back about 750 years. The Royal Oak has been an inn since the 1600s and is located in one of the oldest parts of Appleby. Inside, there are lots of charming old features which enhance the character of this former coaching inn – oak panelled walls and open fires helping to create a cosy, old fashioned atmosphere. The menu has a varied choice of dishes and the inn's ales include Theakstons Best Bitter, Yates Bitter and Premium and Youngers Scotch Bitter. There are also several guest beers. Accommodation includes seven en suite double rooms and two singles. The licensees acquired the cottage next door and converted it into a non-smoking dining room. The Royal Oak received CAMRA's 'Pub of the Year for Cumbria' award several years ago. Times of opening are: 11.00 – 3.00 and 6.00 – 11.00 between Monday and Saturday and 12.00 – 3.00 and 7.00 – 10.30 on Sunday.

Settle – Carlisle Railway

Probably the most famous stretch of regional railway line in Britain, the beauty of its surroundings belies its turbulent past. During the late 1980s the Settle – Carlisle line was under sentence of death when British Rail announced they wanted to close it because of crippling maintenance costs. A desperate rescue plan was launched by armies of train spotters, railway afficionados and Friends of the Settle – Carlisle Line. Eventually, in April 1989, at the eleventh hour, the railway was saved when the Secretary of State for Transport ruled that it must remain open.

Passengers on the Settle – Carlisle Railway are treated to a moving backdrop of wild and breathtaking Pennine scenery. For those who use the line to travel to and from work experience one of the most spectacular train rides in Britain. There may be some truth in the old maxim that familiarity breeds contempt, but, even so, a daily trip on the Settle – Carlisle line must be infinitely preferable to most commuter train journeys! The railway is 72 miles long and is often lined with waving spectators and nostalgia-loving enthusiasts who travel from miles around to gaze in awe at the steam-hauled carriages making their way across this rugged terrain. One of the most fascinating aspects of the railway is its engineering history. One can only gaze in amazement at the graceful Victorian viaducts and bridges, defying the merciless elements and standing as a permanent testimony to the skill and expertise of the men who built them.

Appleby church

Appleby-in-Westmorland

Pleasantly set in the fertile Eden valley, Appleby-in-Westmorland – 'place of the apple tree' – used to be the county town of Westmorland before it became part of Cumbria in the county boundary changes of 1974. 800 years earlier, in 1174, Henry II conferred on Appleby the status of royal borough. The town is a popular base for tourists and holiday-makers and particularly for anglers and walkers. Taking a stroll around Appleby reveals many surprises – the Eden flows prettily through the town, and at the top of Boroughgate is the imposing facade of Appleby castle. The castle, which contains a conservation centre where various rare breeds of farm animals can be seen, is a motte-and-bailey type dating back to the 12th century. It was established by the Normans to guard against a winding, vulnerable stretch of the river. Lady Anne Clifford, whose name crops up frequently in the history of the area, dismantled and restored the castle during the mid-17th century. Lady Anne married several times and her family owned a number of other castles in the Eden valley. Her tomb is in 12th century St Lawrence's church, which can be seen at the bottom of Boroughgate as you leave the castle gate, framed by shops and Georgian houses either side of Low Cross and the 16th century Moot Hall and rising above the Cloisters, rebuilt in 1811. This area of Appleby is probably one of the most picturesque and certainly one of the most photographed.

The Royal Oak

The Walk

1. On leaving the inn bear left and follow the B6542 until you reach a turning on the left for Hilton and Murton. Pass the cemetery and a row of houses. Ahead of you the North Pennines rise spectacularly to meet the skyline. Cross the Settle-Carlisle Railway and then pass under the A66. Once through the bridge bear left towards Flakebridge. Follow the lane down between hedgerows and trees. The routine sounds of the town begin to recede now as you head for unspoilt countryside. The slopes of Dufton Pike can be seen in the distance over to the west. When the lane sweeps round to the right, and just before it begins to climb, turn left through a wooden gate and join a track.

2. Follow the track as it cuts between drystone wall and a wire fence up on the bank on the right. Pass a sign 'no cycling and all dogs must be on a lead' and continue on the track as it cuts across fields bordered by the unattractively named Stank Wood on the left! Pass a waymarked path on the left and continue on the main track beside lines of evergreens on the right. Go through a gate in a boundary wall and then cross over Frith Beck. The track curves now to the right to reach a gate on the edge of Flakebridge Wood.

3. Cross a stile by the gate and bear left signposted Esplandhill. The floor of the woodland here is covered by a luxuriant carpet of bluebells in spring. Follow the track along the edge of the mixed woodland. Silver birch, beech and pine are among the species to be found on this stretch of the walk. Pass to the right of a timber barn and follow the waymarkers beyond it, aiming half-left down to the woodland boundary fence. Follow a narrow path, cross a stile and keep the fence on your right now as you pass under the branches of some overhanging beech trees. At the end of the woodland go through a gate and follow the track as it curves to the left across the fields. Pass through another gate, cross a beck, follow the track round to the right and then between hedgerows up to the farm at Esplandhill.

4. Go down to the road and turn left. As you reach the road note the little methodist church on the right. Pass a turning on the right to Brampton and go on up the hill. Glance back at this stage for a stunning view of the North Pennines. Immediately beyond Clickham Farm on the left, opposite a turning to Milburn and Long Marton, bear left and follow the path alongside the house to a gate at the end of the garden.

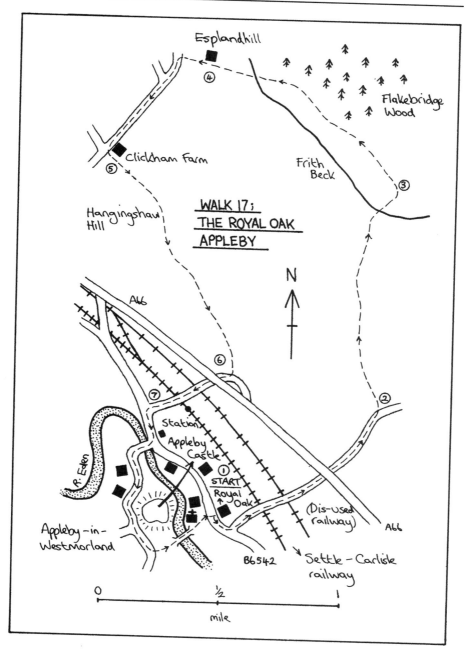

Esplandhill

④

Flakebridge Wood

Clickham Farm

⑤

Frith Beck

③

WALK 17;
THE ROYAL OAK
APPLEBY

Hangingshaw Hill

N
↑

A66

⑥

⑦

②

Station

Appleby Castle

①
START
Royal Oak

R. Eden

(Dis-used railway)

A66

Appleby-in-Westmorland

B6542

Settle-Carlisle railway

0   ½   1

mile

5. Join a rather overgrown path between fences and verges of vegetation. Pass through a gate and walk along a clear track between hedgerows to another gate. Soon the track curves right to become a grassy path leading to a stile. In the next field continue to maintain the same direction, keeping the fence on your left. Make for the stile in the corner, cross the next field by going diagonally right to the top corner. Cross several stiles in quick succession and continue with the field boundary on your right. When you reach a gate at right-angles to you, cross a stile and then go along to the next stile. Join a metalled lane (signposted Brampton and Murton) and look for a footpath on the right to Appleby.

6. Go through the kissing gate and straight across the field to the next boundary. Cross a lane to a stile, down a flight of steps to the A66 and then across it to a flight of steps and a ladder stile. Follow the path ahead towards Appleby town centre. The path joins the road and soon you are passing Appleby primary school and the railway station.

7. At the junction bear left and walk alongside the tree-lined Eden to the next junction. Turn right at this point (signposted Appleby Castle) and then go round to the left into Boroughgate. Pass the church and Moot Hall and head up the hill towards Appleby Castle, noting rows of delightful lime trees. The trees were planted in 1876 by the bell-ringers of St Lawrence's church. Beyond the castle follow the road and the wall, pass Colby Lane and when the road swings right, veer away from it down Castle Bank. Cross Jubilee Bridge over the Eden and then walk up Mill Hill to the road. The inn is on the left.

18. Brough

Route: The Golden Fleece, Brough – Church Brough – Brough Castle – Swindale Beck – Great Musgrave – Lowgill Farm – The Golden Fleece, Brough

Distance: 4½ miles

Map: OS Pathfinder 597, OS Landranger 91

Start: The Golden Fleece, Market Street, Brough

Public transport: There are several bus services serving Brough; X69 and X71 which run between Newcastle and Blackpool; X74 and 560 which operate between Darlington and Carlisle. Nearby Kirkby Stephen is on the Settle – Carlisle railway.

The Golden Fleece, Brough

During the late 17th and early 18th centuries there were almost 20 inns in Brough – The Golden Fleece among them. In the mid-19th century there were plans to build a railway line from Barnard Castle to Penrith via Brough.

The Golden Fleece

Many of the town's hostelries disappeared, however, when it was decided
that the line would by-pass Brough in favour of Kirkby Stephen 4 miles to
the south. The Golden Fleece, which dates back to about 1779 and was
originally a farmhouse, is fortunately one of those inns that has survived the
vagaries of the local economy. Permanent cask conditioned ales include
Boddingtons and Trophy Ale. Food is served every day and accommodation
is also available at the inn. The Golden Fleece is open between 11.00 and 3.00
and 6.00 and 11.00 from Monday to Saturday and 12.00 – 3.00 and 7.00 – 10.30
on Sunday. There is a small car park at the back of the inn and plenty of room
to park elsewhere in the town.

The ruins of Brough Castle

Brough

Brough essentially consists of two distinct halves – Market Brough to the
north and Church Brough to the south. The history of this isolated little town,
bisected by the busy A66, can be traced back over 2,000 years. Most notable
among Brough's ancient buildings are the imposing remains of a Norman
castle. The castle is understood to date back to the 11th century and was
restored in the 17th century by Lady Anne Clifford, who was a significant
figure in the history of this area. Her family also owned castles at nearby

Appleby and Kirkby Stephen. The view from the walk of Brough Castle ruins, set against the splendid backdrop of the hills, is surely one of the most memorable and dramatic in the North Pennines. There is a wildness, a sense of history about this view, evoking colourful romantic images of the castle's past. The remains of Brough Castle are situated immediately to the north east of the Roman fort of Verterae. During the Roman Occupation a military road was constructed between Carlisle and York – and Brough was one of a number of forts strategically positioned along the route of the road chiefly in order to defend it. In its heyday Brough was a coaching town. However, the dawning of the railway era signalled its decline as an important staging post.

The Walk

1. From the front of the inn turn immediately left by the clock tower – a well known landmark in and around Brough. The clock tower is dated 1911 and was moved to its present site to make way for the A66 by-pass a few years ago. Walk down to the A66 and go under the road bridge. The ruins of Brough Castle are visible at this point. Immediately beyond the A66 road bridge join a fenced path leading to Church Brough. The A685 is parallel on the left. Pass Brough county primary school and a bridleway to Musgrave. Further up the hill turn right for Brough Castle. Pass between rows of pretty stone cottages and look for a gate leading into the grounds of the castle.

2. As well as the castle ruins, there are glorious views of the Pennine hills to the north, the buildings of Brough and the Swindale Beck meandering through the countryside below. After visiting the castle return to the main gate and take the lane down to St Michael's church. The present church is 12th century and includes some Roman memorial stones – evidence of the Roman occupation of this area crops up at every turn! An age-old tradition involves children locking the church gates when a wedding is taking place, only allowing guests through when money is offered!

   Follow the lane as it bends to the right of the church. At the fork veer right and go up the steep slope. There are good views of the castle here and the surrounding hills. It is a timeless picture. Among the summits are Wild Boar Fell, rising to 2324 ft. , and Nine Standards, which are cairns constructed, according to legend, to give the impression an English army was camped in the hills, discouraging Scots raiders from advancing.

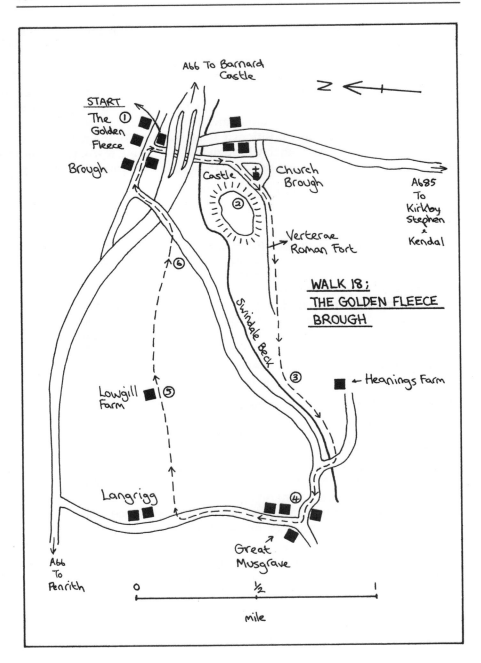

A66 To Barnard Castle

N ←

START
The ① Golden Fleece

Brough

Castle

✝ Church Brough

A685 To Kirkby Stephen & Kendal

②

Verterae Roman Fort

WALK 18;
THE GOLDEN FLEECE
BROUGH

Swindale Beck

⑥

③

Hearings Farm

Lowgill Farm ■ ⑤

④

Langrigg

Great Musgrave

A66 To Penrith

0   ½   1

mile

Keep on along the track over high ground, with magnificent views in all directions. Eventually the track enters a field. Continue to an old byre and immediately beyond it, go through a gate and maintain the same direction. Head across the field in a westerly direction and make for a gap in a line of trees. Aim slightly right to a stile in the far boundary and then emerge on to the bank of the Swindale Beck.

3. Follow the path with the fast-flowing beck on your right. Keep to the broad grassy bank, pass a signposted path to Brough Sowerby and continue to a gate in the next boundary. Join a track to Heanings Farm and turn right for the road. Bear left and follow the lane round to the right into the village of Great Musgrave.

4. Turn right at the junction, by a telephone box, and follow the lane down towards Langrigg. A little over half a mile from Great Musgrave bear right, through a gate (signposted Brough) and follow a track with fencing on the right. Pass through a gate into the next field. Cross it diagonally to a gate. The hills rise up to the northerly horizon – like great slumbering giants. Ahead of you the crumbling remains of Brough Castle peep into view. Head for the buildings of Lowgill Farm, passing two more gates. Join a track when you draw level with the farm, turn left towards the farmhouse, then immediately right into the next field.

5. Cross the field to a wooden gate in the next boundary; walk ahead keeping to the left corner of a barn. Go through a gate beside it and continue ahead to a gate in the next boundary. Keep to the right-hand edge of the field, following the path along the bank. Aim for the corner of the field and drop down to a dilapidated old byre. Cross into the next field and then go straight ahead to the far boundary.

6. Turn left and here you have a choice. Either return to Brough by following the road to the junction, turning right and walking back to the centre of the town, or follow the bridleway parallel to the A66 and join the A685 just to the south of the by-pass. However, this involves crossing the shallow Swindale Beck – which lacks a bridge at this point.

19. Winton

Route: The Bay Horse Inn, Winton – Whingill – Hartley – Kirkby Stephen – River Eden – Eden Place – The Bay Horse Inn, Winton

Distance: 3½ miles

Map: OS Pathfinder 597 and 607, OS Landranger 91

Start: The Bay Horse Inn, Winton. The village is a mile or so to the north of Kirkby Stephen, and is signposted from the A685.

Public transport: Kirkby Stephen is on the Settle–Carlisle Railway. The station is just outside the town. Bus services X69, X71 and 560 serve Kirkby Stephen, calling also at Barnard Castle, Bowes and Brough.

The Bay Horse, Winton (017683 71451)

The Bay Horse was quite probably built as a farmhouse and barn in the 1670s. It has been an inn for a great many years and at one time the dray

horse for Kirkby Stephen brewery was kept here. Inside, there are two quaint bars with low ceilings and photographs of Pennine scenes. Home-cooked food is available every day, there are snacks throughout the day in summer and the traditional ales include Jennings Ordinary Bitter, Theakstons Best and Youngers Scotch Bitter. There are also several guest beers. The inn includes accommodation and the times of opening are as follows: Summer 12.00 – 11.00 – Winter 12.00 – 2.00 and 6.30 – 11.00. Sunday hours throughout the year are 12.00 – 3.00 and 7.00 – 10.30.

Kings Arms Hotel, Kirkby Stephen (017683 71378)

The Kings Arms is a rambling old 17th century former Posting Inn and includes an old fashioned oak-panelled lounge bar, an attractive dining room decorated with antique furniture and tapestries, and an ancient Powder Closet. Cask ales include Whitbread, Boddingtons and Trophy, food is available every day and the times of opening are 11.00 – 3.00 and 6.00 – 11.00 between Monday and Saturday and 12.00 – 3.00 and 7.00 – 10.30 on Sunday.

Winton

During the 19th century Winton was a thriving village with a great many more shops and businesses than you see today. The premises of several grocers, a blacksmith, a tailor, a dressmaker and two joiners overlooked the pretty green at the centre of Winton. There were also four schools here. Winton has always been a farming community – though there are fewer working farms now than during the period of Winton's greatest prosperity. In the locality there is evidence of the old agricultural practice of strip farming.

Kirkby Stephen

This pleasant little market town lies in the upper Eden valley and is on the route of the spectacular 'Coast to Coast' walk – pioneered by Alfred Wainwright and extending the width of England between St Bees on the Cumbrian west coast and Robin Hood's Bay on the Yorkshire east coast. The town is a bustling place with a youth hostel and many small hotels and guest houses. In summer its population increases, as visitors, using Kirkby Stephen as a touring base, stroll its streets and along the banks of the pretty Eden. Kirkby Stephen is also a favourite haunt of anglers. In the evening, in the town's inns and hotels, you can easily find yourself striking up conversations, as I have done, with those tackling Wainwright's splendid route.

Kirkby Stephen's history is based on wool and local agriculture. At one time a butter market operated in the town's Cloisters, built in the early 19th century by a local man. The historic 13th century church of St Stephen, often described as the 'Cathedral of the Dales', contains the tomb of Sir Richard Musgrave who was alleged to have slain Cumbria's last wild boar in the area. A boar's husk was found in his tomb. Kirkby Stephen upholds the local tradition of ringing a curfew or taggy bell on some occasions. This is a warning to those staying out late that they may be swooped on by the 'Taggy' – considered by some of Kirkby Stephen's children to be a demon.

Kirkby Stephen church

The Walk

1. From the front of the pub turn left and walk down the lane. As you leave the village of Winton, a footpath sign for Eden Place comes into view on the right. This represents the final leg of the walk. Follow the lane and after about 60 yards or so it forks. Bear left (signposted Hartley). When you reach a solitary beech tree on the left, leave the road and take the path signposted to Hartley. Look back at this point for a stunning view of Winton with the Pennine chain rising majestically to the horizon. Over to the west the towering peaks of the Lake District can be seen in the far distance. Keep close to the left-hand boundary and cross the stone stile into the next field. Head diagonally right to the gate in the field corner. In the next field go forward to join a track taking you to the buildings of Whingill – an old Norse term for 'gorse ravine'. Cross a stile and when you draw level with the house, bear right.

2. Follow the track in a south-westerly direction and once more you are treated to panoramic views of the Eden valley and the Pennine summits. Dufton Pike and the high points of Great Dun Fell and Cross Fell can be spotted here. As you descend the track you can also see the houses of Kirkby Stephen ahead. Pass an old byre and at the road turn left. Pass a turning to Kirkby Stephen and continue along the lane to the centre of Hartley. Pass rows of picturesque cottages and a scurrying beck; at a telephone box join the lane running parallel to the main street.

3. Follow it until you reach Saltpie Hall. Turn right immediately beyond it to join a path running between drystone walls. Ahead of you is the church tower at Kirkby Stephen. Follow the path down towards the town. Go through a wooden kissing gate and along a path beside the swirling Eden. Cross the river at the stone bridge. This is known as Frank's Bridge.

4. Go up the flight of steps, bearing right at the top to follow the lane round to the church and the town centre. On leaving Kirkby Stephen take the alleyway beside Barclay's Bank and return to Frank's Bridge. Cross it and then go through the kissing gate on the left. Head along the edge of the sports fields, keeping the Eden over to your left. Eventually, in the field corner, you reach a footbridge spanning the gushing waters of Hartley Beck. Head out to the road and go straight along to Low Mill Bridge. Join the riverside path on the right-hand

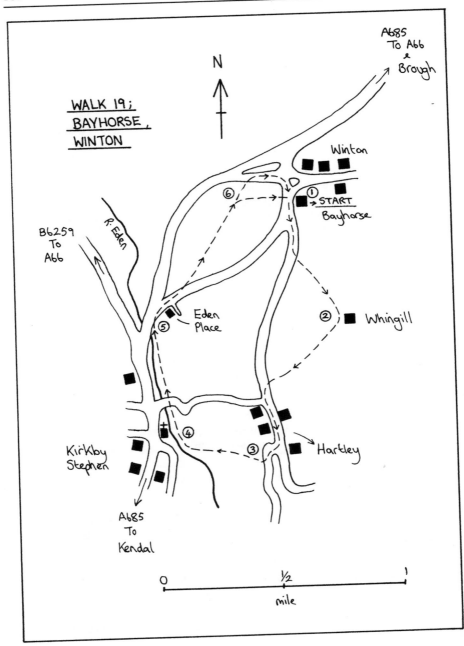

WALK 19;
BAYHORSE,
WINTON

bank (signposted New Bridge). The path is low-lying and can be wet and muddy in places but the stretches under the overhanging branches of elm, alder and sycamore trees are very pleasant. Soon the route is along the edge of a rectangular field and in the corner you cross a burn to reach the main A685.

5. Turn right and walk along the road until you come to a turning on the right to Winton. Walk down the lane, under some beech trees, and pass the turning to Eden Place. After about 70 yards cross a stile on the left (signposted Winton). Swing half-right to a stile in the next boundary. Follow a vague path obliquely right to the next boundary. Aim slightly left and beyond the next stile keep to the right-hand boundary of the field. Beyond the next stile, aim a little to the left to a stone stile near a line of power cables. Aim half-left to a stile at the corner of a wood consisting of birch, ash and hawthorn trees. Kestrels and hawks are known to frequent the area. Cross Mill Beck, then go left towards the houses of Winton. Beyond a line of beeches you have a choice.

6. Turn right and cross the fields to a farm beyond which is the road and the inn where the walk began. To see a little more of the village, continue ahead at the line of beech trees to reach the road after about 60 yards. Turn right and walk back to the pub.

20. High Force

Route: The High Force Hotel – Wat Garth – Forest-in-Teesdale – Widdy Bank Farm – Cronkley – High Force – The High Force Hotel

Distance: 9½ miles

Map: OS Outdoor Leisure 31 (Teesdale), OS Landranger 92

Start: The High Force Hotel on the B6277, north of Middleton-in-Teesdale. Follow the signs for High Force. The inn is opposite the entrance to the famous Teesdale beauty spot and adjacent to its car park.

Public transport: Bus services 75/76 operate between Darlington and Langdon Beck, calling at the High Force Hotel.

The High Force Hotel (01833 22222)

This rambling old inn was originally an 18th century shooting lodge for the Dukes of Cleveland. Inside, is an old black and white photograph of The Royal Shooting Party – dated 1866. It was taken outside the hotel and includes an impressive line-up of aristocracy. Among them is the Prince of Wales. The High Force quite probably became an inn and hotel soon after this photograph was taken. The present landlord and his wife travelled the world before settling down to run the hotel. Newspaper clippings of their exploits adorn the walls. Food is available here every day and among the real ales are Theakstons Best Bitter, XB and Newcastle Exhibition Ale. There are also several guest beers. The hotel is well known in Teesdale and its customers are usually a mixture of locals, farmers, tourists and walkers. Upstairs there are nine en suite bedrooms. The car park can get very busy, in which case use the adjoining car park for High Force. It is free between November and Easter. The hotel's times of opening are 11.00 – 4.00 and 7.00 – 11.00 between Monday and Saturday and 12.00 – 3.00 and 7.00 – 10.30 on Sunday. Afternoon tea is served from 2.00 – 5.00.

Upper Teesdale

This rugged, spectacular dale is one of the most botanical areas in the country, where a curious sugar limestone crumbles to create a thin alkaline soil which produces a profusion of rich and varied flora, but cannot support dense grass cover. It is commonly believed that many of these rare alpine plants – spring gentian and yellow primrose among them – are remnants of the Ice Age. Incredibly, the seeds of some of them may be millions of years old. Those fascinated by our natural history and geology will undoubtedly find much to distract them on this walk. Upper Teesdale includes a National Nature Reserve, rising to 2,500 feet, where years of painstaking research by experts in the field have helped us to understand and interpret what shapes and influences the land.

Dotted about this majestic landscape are various whitewashed cottages and dwellings. The story goes that the then Lord Barnard, a local landowner, was out shooting on the moors. Fog came down quite suddenly and he was soon lost. He made for a local farmhouse, believing it to be occupied by one of his tenants. He was mistaken – the farmer turned Lord Barnard away, telling him that the property was not on his land. In order to ensure this never happened again, he went home and instructed all the properties on his land be painted white so that he could recognise them immediately in future.

The High Force Hotel

High Force

The Walk

1. Leave the hotel, turn right and walk along the B6277. Bear left at a sign for Hargreaves Quarries and Middleton Quarry (no access for vehicles) and follow the lane. Look to the left at this point and you can see the whitened facade of the High Force Hotel nestling among the trees. Sweeps of moorland rise above it, creating a spectacular picture. Pass a small walled enclosure on the right and then take the track immediately beyond it up towards the farm buildings at Force Garth. Pass to the left of the buildings and go on beside a cottage and some buildings. After almost 200 yards you come to a gate. A sign here advises you to 'Beware of the Bull'. Bear left and cross the rough moorland ground with the wall on your left. Soon there is a magnificent view ahead of Upper Teesdale. The Tees meanders under dramatic scars and windswept fells. Whitewashed dwellings speck the craggy limestone landscape. Drop down to a gate in the far boundary, then bear left towards the river. Veer right after about 150 yards to reach another gate. Drop down the slope, cross a track leading to a farmstead on the left, go through a gate in front of you and follow a track for about 50 yards. Pass through a gap in the wall on the right and then head diagonally left up to another farmstead. Go through a gate and then bear left in front of the house. This is Wat Garth.

2. Turn right in front of the burn and then head for the top of the enclosure. Go through the gate in the right corner, reach another gate after about 60 yards, cross the burn and follow the grassy track as it sweeps up to the right of a house — Birk Rigg. Beyond the house join the main track leading to the road. Turn left and follow it until you come to a track running off half-left down to a whitewashed single-storey dwelling. Follow the track down through the gate. On reaching the building pass through the gate to the right of it, cross the field by going diagonally left to a gate in the boundary, just beyond a telegraph pole with a transformer attached to it. Turn right and follow the boundary wall on the right of you. In the corner go through the gap and then cross into the right-hand field. Walk along the field edge with the wall on your left. Join a track and bear left. Pass through a white gate and follow it round to the right. Soon the track crosses the Langdon Beck and here is a sign telling you that this is the Pennine Way. From here it is 121 miles to Kirk Yetholm in the north and 149 miles to Edale — the southern point of the national trail.

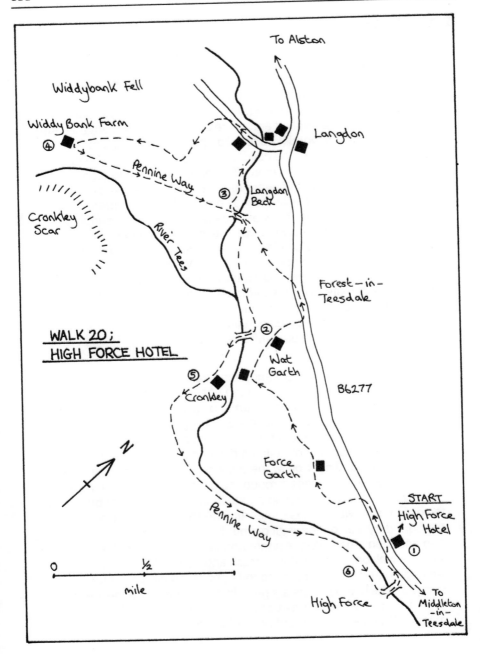

To Alston

Widdybank Fell

Widdy Bank Farm

④

Langdon

Pennine Way

③

Langdon Beck

Cronkley Scar

River Tees

WALK 20;
HIGH FORCE HOTEL

②

Wat Garth

Forest-in-Teesdale

⑤

Cronkley

B6277

N

Force Garth

Pennine Way

START
High Force Hotel
①

0   ½   1
         mile

⑥

High Force

To Middleton-in-Teesdale

3. Bear right over the bridge, cross the gate in the next boundary and continue beside the river. Cross a stone stile further on along the bank and then follow the path through the grounds of a cottage. Turn right at a concrete bridge, then left at the road in front of Beckfoot, a cottage. Follow the road over the water, cross a cattle-grid and then turn left for Cauldron Snout. Rising in front of you is the massive bulk of Cronkley Scar. Follow the track through this stunning landscape — this is some of the wildest scenery in the North Pennines; glorious in summer, savage and hostile in the depths of winter. Pass over a cattle-grid and walk on to the buildings of Widdy Bank Farm.

4. Pass between the farm buildings, through several gates and on down the track to the next gate. Bear sharp left at this point, hard by the Tees, to cross a stone stile. Begin the return leg of the walk here, following the route of the Pennine Way. Cross several rough pastures with the river on your right and Widdy Bank Farm over to your left. Pass through a gate and continue ahead above the river. Cross a stone stile and as the river curves away to the right, the route of the walk is straight ahead along a clear grassy path. Cross the next boundary and at the next one is an information board relating to Upper Teesdale National Nature Reserve. Cross the field diagonally right, over a footbridge and up to the next boundary. Head down the slope, keeping to the right of a farm. Cross the bridge over the Langdon Beck, encountered on the outward leg of the walk, and turn right to follow the riverbank. Pass the confluence of the Tees and the Langdon Beck and continue along the riverside path — still on the Pennine Way. At the next bridge cross to the opposite bank and follow the track towards Cronkley Farm.

5. Just before the farm buildings bear right to join a waymarked path down to the field corner. Cross the stile and bear right to head up between High Crag and Low Crag. At the top there are far-reaching views over Teesdale. Look for a drystone wall on the right. Turn left and follow the boundary, keeping the wall on your left. In the corner bear left over a stile. Head obliquely right up the slope to a waymarker. From this point there are 360-degree views over the North Pennines. Down below, the river snakes through Teesdale. Follow the rock-strewn path as it drops down to the riverbank and cuts between juniper bushes. Pass over various tributary burns and on the left are unsightly quarry works. Soon the trees thicken as you approach High Force.

6. It is claimed that High Force is the highest waterfall in England and is certainly one of the most popular beauty spots in the North Pennines. The boiling, churning water plunges in spectacular fashion over the Whin Sill volcanic rock to a dark, deep pool 70 feet below. Standing on the cliff above the water, you can feel the dank spray on your face. Don't go too near — it's a long way down! There is a stunning view of High Force a little further along the path. The hotel where the walk started is visible on the opposite bank. Continue to a gate and abut 30 yards beyond it drop down the bank to a footbridge. Cross the Tees, then bear left into a pretty meadow. At the end of the meadow go through a gate and up a flight of steps to the road. The High Force Hotel can be seen ahead.

21. Middleton-in-Teesdale

Route: The Foresters Arms, Middleton-in-Teesdale – Pennine Way – River Tees – Newbiggin – Bell House – The Foresters Arms, Middleton-in-Teesdale

Distance: 6 miles

Map: OS Outdoor Leisure 31 (Teesdale), OS Landranger 92

Start: The Foresters Arms, Middleton-in-Teesdale.

Public transport: The village is on several bus routes – including X89, 75 and 76.

The Foresters Arms, Middleton-in-Teesdale (01833 640836)

The Foresters Arms is one of the oldest inns in the village and dates back to the early part of the 19th century. John Smiths is the permanent real ale, food is served every day and there is a beer garden. The inn does not have its own car park but there is plenty of room to park in Middleton-in-Teesdale. The pub is open between 11.00 and 11.00 from Monday to Saturday and 12.00 – 3.00 and 7.00 – 10.30 on Sunday.

The Foresters Arms

Middleton's famous drinking fountain

Middleton-in-Teesdale

Middleton-in-Teesdale, or Middleton as it is known locally, has always been closely associated with the lead mining industry. The London Lead Company, owned and run by Quakers, established its North of England headquarters in the village in the 18th century. Apart from Middleton House, its local office, the company also built homes for the miners as well as a school, library and chapel. As a major local employer, mindful of the needs and welfare of its workers, the London Lead Company encouraged innovation and endorsed ideas of town planning and social harmony.

Take a stroll round the streets of Middleton, designated a Conservation Area, and among other features you may stumble upon is the cast iron drinking fountain in the village centre. Erected in 1875, it commemorates one man's loyalty to the London Lead Company. Robert Bainbridge was the company's superintendent and when he retired, funds to pay for the fountain were raised by his colleagues.

Middleton's focal point is its broad, grassy, tree-lined main street overlooked by rows of shops and old coaching inns. Today, the village is a popular tourist attraction in upper Teesdale as well as a welcome watering hole for those tackling the Pennine Way.

The Walk

1. Leave the inn and turn right. Further along the street bear right into Bridge Street, the B6277, signposted Scotch Corner. Pass Middleton-in-Teesdale Field Studies Centre and on the left is the Teesdale Way. Cross the Tees and pass beside Middleton Farmers' Market. Just beyond it turn right to join the route of the Pennine Way. Follow the track through various gates and over some stiles. The route is clear and unmistakable – hardly surprising as you are walking a stretch of one of Britain's most popular national trails! The Tees snakes through the Teesdale landscape and is never far from the path. Soon the Pennine Way runs high above the river and then swings away from it to cut between fields and drystone walls. Pass signs of a disused quarry works on the left and continue to the higher ground. There are good views down over the river and its upper Teesdale setting.

2. On the opposite bank is the white facade of the farm at Low Houses. Woodside Farm can be seen further up the slopes to the north of it. All along this stretch of the Pennine Way are glorious glimpses of

Teesdale between the trees. Follow the waymarkers down through the trees, cross a burn feeding into the Tees, then some stepping stones over another tributary to continue along the riverside path.

3. Follow the Pennine Way until you reach Scoberry Bridge over the Tees. Cross the river at this point, go through the gate by a barn and then aim for the corner of the next field, where there are some trees. Follow the footbridge over the pretty Bow Lee Beck. Emerge from the trees and follow the path across the fields towards the buildings of Newbiggin. At the road turn right, then bear left after about 40 yards. Follow the lane towards white-painted Fellowship Farm and then swing right at the first junction. This is Newbiggin, first recorded as a village as far back as 1200. In the 18th century Newbiggin grew in stature as a direct result of the lead-mining era. Many miners lived and worked in the area and the village had its own smelter.

4. Cross the beck, pass Newbiggin Methodist chapel, dated 1759, and continue through the village. Ascend the steep slope and follow the road as it bends steeply and sharply to the left. At this point look for a stone stile by a wrought iron gate. Once in the field make for a ladder stile in the left boundary wall. Swing half-right to the next wall, then swing obliquely left to a ladder stile taking you into some peaceful woodland. Follow the path between the trees and banks of wild flowers. Go up a short, steep bank to a junction of paths and bear right by a wooded gully. Pass over another ladder stile and Low Houses, seen on the outward leg of the walk, can now be spotted down in the valley. Cross the boundary into the next field, then begin to veer slightly left and up the field slope towards the buildings of Bell House. Look for a stone stile in the boundary and pass to the left of the house. Cross another stile, then turn left and go out to the road.

5. Bear right and follow this quiet lane. On the right are breathtaking views over a wide expanse of Teesdale. Eventually you reach the junction with the B6277. Continue ahead and back into the centre of Middleton.

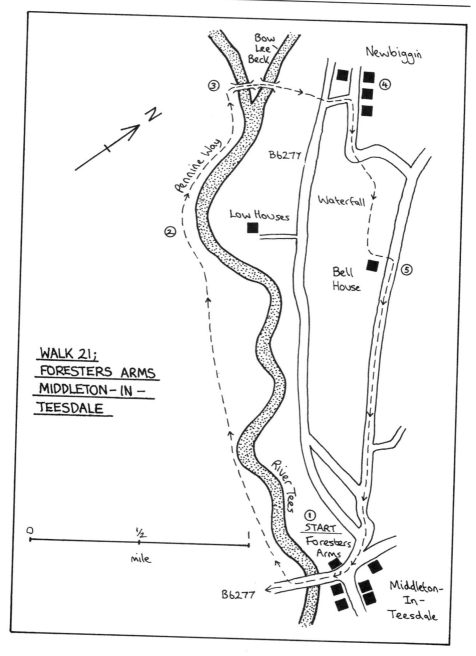

Bow Lee Beck

Newbiggin

③

④

Pennine Way

Bb277

Waterfall

Low Houses

②

Bell House

⑤

WALK 21;
FORESTERS ARMS
MIDDLETON - IN -
TEESDALE

River Tees

①
START
Foresters
Arms

Middleton-
In -
Teesdale

Bb277

0   ½   1
            mile

22. Cotherstone

Route: The Fox and Hounds, Cotherstone – St Cuthbert's Church – Butter Stone – Corn Park – River Balder – The Fox and Hounds, Cotherstone

Distance: 4¼ miles

Map: OS Outdoor Leisure 31 (Teesdale), OS Landranger 92

Start: The Fox and Hounds, Cotherstone. The village is about 3½ miles north-west of Barnard Castle, on the B6277.

Public transport: Several buses stop at Cotherstone, including service 75, which runs between Darlington and Middleton-in-Teesdale.

The Fox and Hounds, Cotherstone (01833 650241)

Overlooking the pretty village green and close to the rivers Tees and Balder, the Fox and Hounds has been a beamed coaching inn for more than 200 years. The inn features in several tourist guides to local inns and hotels. The pub also uses local Cotherstone cheese as a stuffing for breast of chicken. Inside, the inn has a welcoming atmosphere. There are lots of nooks and crannies and the heavily beamed bar includes a log fire, several alcoves and recesses. There are also lots of photographs and prints of rural scenes lining the walls. The Fox and Hounds has an excellent reputation for food and also includes accommodation. Among the beers on handpump are John Smiths Cask Bitter and two local brews – Hambleton Best Bitter and White Boar Bitter. Times of opening are 11.30 – 2.30 and 6.30 – 11.00 between Monday and Saturday and 12.00 – 2.30 and 7.00 – 10.30 on Sunday.

Cotherstone

The village is a long straggling community with its roots deep in agriculture. The main street, lined with endless rows of stone cottages, seems to go on forever. There was a 12th century castle at Cotherstone but today only one or two mounds can be seen. Hannah Hauxwell, a true local Daleswoman who became something of a media celebrity through a series of television documentaries and books, has lived in and around the village for a number of years.

The opening of the Tees Valley Railway in the 19th century brought renewed prosperity to Cotherstone and it quickly became a favoured base for touring Teesdale and other parts of the region. The railway closed in the mid-1960s but the village, which has been designated a Conservation Area, continues to be a popular choice for tourists and visitors. The famous Cotherstone cheese is made in the locality.

Crossing the River Balder

The Butter Stone

Isolated amid the moors outside Cotherstone, the Butter Stone is a well known local and ancient landmark which dates back to the Great Plague of 1665-66. Such was the fear of infection that money to buy farm produce, including butter, was coated in vinegar to act as a disinfectant substance. The hollow in the stone was where the cash was placed.

The Walk

1. From the inn turn right and walk along the main street of the village. Pass the county junior and infants school and follow the road as it curves to the right. At a sharp left bend go straight on towards St Cuthbert's church. Beyond the church follow the road over a cattle grid and begin to head out across the open moorland.

2. Keep to the road as it bends left. Further up is a magnificent view behind you of Cotherstone and its glorious Teesdale setting. The trees protect the Tees and the Balder at the point where the two rivers meet. Continue up the road as it climbs the moorland slopes. On the horizon is the outline of a public bridleway sign, which you should make for. On reaching it, on the crest of the hill, just beyond the flat roofed waterworks building and a white gate, swing right and follow the bridleway.

3. On the right here is the Butter Stone, nestling amidst the heather and tussock grass. Follow the track and ahead of you in the distance is Booze Wood. Keep on the track as it descends into a dip and cross Crook Beck. Beyond it veer half-right and aim for a gate immediately to the left of a copse. Pass through the gate and walk down beside the woodland enclosing a stone cottage. This has the delightful name of Cuckoo. Ahead of you now is a magnificent view of Teesdale; a vast and majestic landscape of rolling moorland and woods. Go through a gate and down beside various fields and enclosures. Beyond another gate bear sharp left and at Corn Park, a farm, pass through a gate and then turn right just beyond the house.

4. Drop down the track to some trees at the road side. Cross over and into the field by an old corrugated hay barn. Walk down beside the Osmond Beck. At the bottom of the field cross the stile into the trees. Follow the path and take particular care along this stretch. The path can be very wet and slippery in places. Further on a fence helps you down to a footbridge over the Balder — named after a Viking God. The river is particularly scenic at this point, racing through the spectacular wooded gorge. The Balder and its surrounding woodland are important wildlife habitats, with dippers and kingfishers known to frequent the area.

5. Go up the bank to a stile and follow the waymarker. At the top of the steep slope join a track and veer right. Follow the track as it curves left and crosses a beck. 20 yards beyond it swing right to a gate and

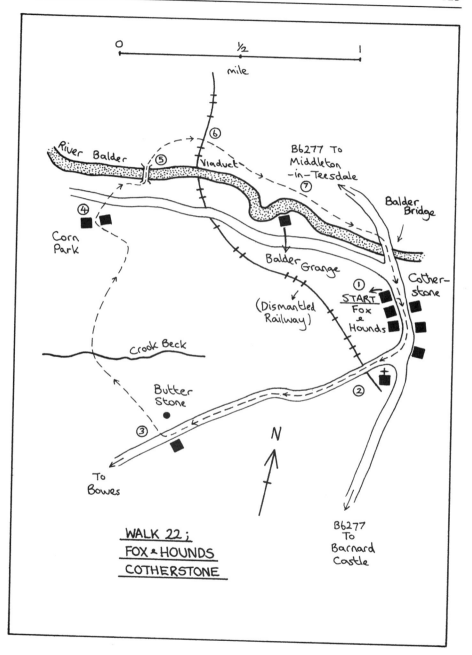

WALK 22 ;
FOX & HOUNDS
COTHERSTONE

waymarker. Walk along the well used path under some power cables. On the right now is the viaduct on the old disused Barnard Castle to Middleton-in-Teesdale railway line. The imposing structure has nine arches and was built in 1868.

6. Cross the route of the old line via several concrete ladder stiles. Head across the field, cross the next boundary and continue to a stile. Cross the field and then through a line of trees into the next field. Make for two gates in the far corner. Avoid the gate by the trees and take the one by the stile.

7. On the right now is the Elizabethan facade of Balder Grange, overlooking the river. The rocky, tree-lined gorge is still far below you. Cross into the next field and keep to its right-hand boundary. Cross a stile in the field corner, then another stile, drop down to a gate. Head diagonally across the field to the far boundary and out to the road. Turn right, crossing the Balder by some beech trees. The bridge here has been rebuilt more than once and originally dates back to the 15th century. The Fox and Hounds is a little further on along the village street.

The Fox and Hounds

23. Barnard Castle

Route: The Old Well Inn, Barnard Castle – Wyse Hill Farm – Egglestone Abbey – Bowes Museum – The Old Well Inn, Barnard Castle

Distance: 5¾ miles

Map: OS Outdoor Leisure 31 (Teesdale), OS Landranger 92

Start: The Old Well is in the centre of Barnard Castle, on The Bank, once the town's main commercial thoroughfare.

Public transport: Barnard Castle is on the route of many bus services, including X69, X71, X74, 8, 75, 76, 495 and 560.

The Old Well Inn, Barnard Castle (01833 690130)

The Old Well was for many years a locally famous coaching inn. In more recent times it became known as the Railway Hotel. The surprising discovery of a well in the vaulted cellars led to the inn's name being changed. The Old Well has three en-suite bedrooms, a range of home-cooked food and a children's menu available every day. There is also the adjoining Rabanas Restaurant. Among the ales on handpump are Courage Directors, John Smiths and Boddingtons Bitter. The inn does not have a car park but there is ample room to park in the town. Times of opening are 12.00 – 2.00 and 7.00 – 11.00 between Monday and Saturday and 12.00 – 2.00 and 7.00 – 10.30 on Sunday.

Barnard Castle

A fine market town guarded by its imposing Norman castle, built by Guy de Bailleul to defend a vital river crossing. The impressive ruins, creating a striking picture against the skyline, rise above a cliff overlooking the Tees. Warwick the Kingmaker acquired the castle during the 15th century. It passed by marriage to Richard III. The castle is in the care of English Heritage and open to the public. The remains include parts of the 14th century great hall and a cylindrical 12th century tower.

Charles Dickens stayed at the King's Head in Barnard Castle in 1838 whilst researching 'Nicholas Nickleby'. If time allows, take a stroll round the town and you cannot fail to be impressed by its quaint streets and period buildings. Look out for the octagonal Market Cross built in 1747.

Barnard Castle

Egglestone Abbey

The crumbling remains are all that is left of a Premonstratensian abbey founded in about 1196 and now administered by English Heritage. The abbey, prettily located on the south bank of the Tees, blends into this green and fertile landscape. Part of the cruciform church is still intact. Many of the old monastic buildings became private dwellings following the Dissolution. Turner was inspired to paint the famous view of the abbey and its riverside setting.

Bowes Museum

Built originally by the French architect Jules Pellachet, this French-style chateau stands incongruously amid traditional stone buildings on the outskirts of Barnard Castle. Its opulent splendour is almost breathtaking and if you are not familiar with its historical background, you could be forgiven for asking how on earth it came to be here. In fact it was John Bowes, the son of the 10th Earl of Strathmore, who was inspired to build it for his French wife Josephine, an actress. Sadly, both of them died before construction work was finished. Both Bowes and his wife intended the magnificent building to house a museum and eventually, in 1892, the official unveiling ceremony took place. Today, the museum contains collections of furniture, ceramics, clocks, tapestries and the largest display of French and Spanish paintings. Run by Durham County Council, the museum is open daily.

The Old Well

The Walk

1. Emerge from the Old Well, turn right and walk down the street. When the road bends sharp right, go straight on into Thorngate. On the left is an old woollen factory built in the mid-19th century and the last industrial waterside building to be completed in Barnard Castle. A plaque recalls its history in some detail. Follow the late 18th century footbridge over the Tees and then up the slope to the junction by a wall. Bear right and at this stage of the walk there is a wide view over the rooftops of Barnard Castle. At the road swing left for several yards, then turn right for Boldron. The castle ruins are visible now, rising above the river. Pass Holy Trinity church in the village of Startforth and at the next junction, bear left.

2. Follow the road beside Hall Farm and pass a turning on the right to Wyse Hill Farm. Continue for about 150 yards, then, as the road begins to curve right, pass through the first of two gates. Follow the right-hand boundary of the field. Pass through the gate into the next field and continue towards a line of trees in the dip. Make for the stile amid the trees and continue in the next field. Cross several stiles in quick succession and aim for the field corner. Cross the field to the next boundary, cross some stepping stones over a beck, then head towards a byre. The A66 is not far away, the sound of traffic audible now.

3. Draw level with the byre and swing left to join muddy tracks through several field boundaries. Aim for a stile in a hedgerow, cross three lines of trees and bushes and then make for a stile ahead. Veer half-right to the corner of Princess Charlotte Wood. Cross another stile and follow the right-hand edge of the wood. Go over a stile in the south-east corner of the woodland and then after several yards, bear left over another stile. Swing immediately right now and follow the field boundary to a gate. Join a track and walk along to the B6277.

4. Cross over to a stile into the trees. Beyond them bear half-left across a field to yet another stile. Follow the waymarker obliquely right towards woodland. Make for a stile in the boundary and then walk ahead with the trees on your left. Cross a stile in the field corner and then swing left by the trees. Walk down to the corner of the woodland and then through a gate into the next field. Turn right and immediately you have crossed into the next field, bear left and follow the path over several field boundaries down towards Egglestone Abbey. Join a farm lane and at the road junction, turn right. Egglestone Abbey is now just ahead of you.

5. Pass the abbey and walk down to the junction by the BT telephone box. Bear right here and then left at the medieval packhorse bridge. There is a glorious view of the dark river scurrying far below. Take care here — the bridge is narrow and often busy with passing traffic! On the far side of the bridge is a sign on the left for the Teesdale Way. Take the path and follow it between banks of wild flowers, cow parsley, nettles etc. Go through a gate and across a meadow to another gate. On the left now the ruins of Egglestone Abbey can be seen on a bluff on the far side of the Tees. Cross another boundary and continue on the riverside path. Join a track alongside the Tees

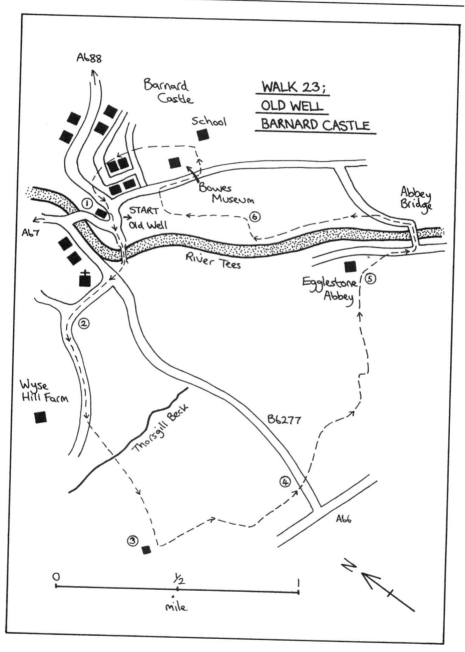

A688

Barnard
Castle

School

WALK 23;
OLD WELL
BARNARD CASTLE

Bowes
Museum

Abbey
Bridge

① START
Old Well

A67

⑥

River Tees

Egglestone
Abbey

⑤

②

Wyse
Hill Farm

Thorsgill Beck

B6277

④

③

A66

0   ½   1
mile

N

and pass the boundary of the water treatment works on the right. Pass through a gate and veer right to a squeeze stile.

6. Beyond it swing half-left to pass under some power lines. Aim for a gate with some playing fields on the left. Continue towards the trees ahead, cross a stile and on the right now is a stunning view of the Bowes Museum. Follow the path alongside the boundary wall, cross another stile and beyond it veer right to the road junction. Turn right by Spring Lodge Hotel and walk along beside Bowes Museum. Beyond the entrance follow the wall until you reach the entrance to Barnard Castle School. Turn left here and follow the road between the school and the museum. The road curves left by the school buildings. Pass a rear entrance to the museum. Further on is Dawson Road on the right. When the road bends sharp left, go straight on to the right of some stone-built houses. Follow the path through the cemetery and at the road turn left. Bear right by Barnard Castle United Reformed Church and return to the centre of the town.

24. Staindrop

Route: The Royal Oak, Staindrop—Friar Cote—Woodend Farm—Sudburn Beck—Snotterton Hall—The Royal Oak, Staindrop

Distance: 6¼ miles

Map: OS Pathfinder 580 and 599, OS Landranger 92

Start: The Royal Oak is in the main street of Staindrop. The village is on the A688, to the north-east of Barnard Castle.

Public transport: Staindrop is on the route of several regular bus services operating between Barnard Castle, Bishop Auckland and Darlington.

The Royal Oak, Staindrop (01833 660281)

The Royal Oak, which dates back to the 1800s, has the feel of a locals' town pub. It is a tall, listed building, and the lounge bar is long and narrow with various beams and horse brasses. At one time it was one of more than a dozen pubs in Staindrop. Now only three remain in the village. Worthington is available on handpump and food is available every day except Sunday. There is also a children's menu. The Royal Oak does not have its own car park but there is plenty of room to park in the village. Times of opening are 12.00 – 5.00 and 7.00 – 11.00 between Monday and Saturday and 12.00 – 3.00 and 7.00 – 10.30 on Sunday.

Staindrop

Staindrop is most closely associated with Raby Castle, which lies just to the north of this long, straggling village. Staindrop is Danish in origin – 'Standropa' means stony place. The church is Saxon and contains several splendid monuments to the Neville family who owned Raby Castle. Staindrop's single street includes a tree-lined green and an assortment of 17th and 18th century houses and cottages. Until the end of the 18th century, there was a weekly market in the village, which has been designated a Conservation Area to help preserve its charming mellowstone buildings.

The green at Staindrop

Raby Castle

The 11th century castle, which was the family seat of the Nevilles for two centuries, stands in magnificent parkland extending to nearly 300 acres, with several lakes, gardens and a deer park. Perhaps one of the castle's most unusual features is the Neville gateway, which enabled carriages to drive into the castle and draw up at an inner stair. There are also nine individual towers – the highest of which is 80 ft. History was made at Raby in November 1569 when the Rising of the North – designed to install Mary on the throne in place of Queen Elizabeth – was plotted here in the great Baron's Hall. The plan failed and the medieval castle was subsequently acquired by the Vanes in 1626. Sir Henry Vane, a descendant, held Raby for Parliament at the time of the English Civil War. He was later tried as a traitor and executed in the Tower of London. Raby's octagonal drawing room is considered to be one of the finest Victorian drawing rooms in the country. The castle, which also contains furniture, paintings and ceramics among other treasures, is open to the public at certain times.

The Walk

1. Leave the inn by turning right and walking along the main A688 towards North Green. Skirt the pretty green, pass a telephone box and then veer over to the right to Lady Close. Take the footpath at the side of a row of cottages and follow it between walls all the way to the hedge. Keep the hedge on the right until you reach a gap. Once through it maintain the same direction. This narrow path is known as 'Knicky Nack'. Cross into the next field and then continue along the thin path to a gap stile. Veer a little to the right in the next field, towards the boundary wall of Raby Park. Make for the far corner of the field, cross several field boundaries with the wall and Raby Wood on your right. Soon you reach one of the lodges to the estate.

2. Pass the lodge and keep alongside the boundary wall to the next lodge by some wrought iron fencing and stone gate pillars. The date on the side of the lodge is 1914. Continue with the boundary wall on the right and pass a gate in the wall. Peering through the opening reveals a dazzling picture. Bluebells thrive in colourful profusion beneath the overhanging branches of beech trees. When the woodland ends continue alongside the wall and soon you come to a track. There are good views at this point across the wooded Raby estate.

3. Turn left and walk up to the road. Bear right and follow the B6279. In summer the verges and surrounding fields are bright yellow with dandelions. Keep to the road until you come to a footpath on the left (signposted Friar Cote). Follow the track down to the farm buildings and go through the gate to the right of Friar Cote Cottage.

4. Head down the right-hand boundary of the field towards some barns. Pass through the gate beside them and then go straight ahead towards the field corner. Stay inside the field boundary and bear left towards some trees. Follow the path alongside Lingberry Quarry and its pretty woodland. Go up to the next gate and then cross the field diagonally, down to the bottom corner where there is a gate. Follow the boundary wall of Streatlam Park on your right. Pass through three gates and, beyond the boundary wall, begin to approach the buildings of Woodend Farm.

5. Cross the stile by the farm, go over the track and follow the waymarkers. Cross another stile and walk alongside the Sudburn Beck. Cross several field boundaries to reach the buildings of Streatlam Grove Farm. Go down the bank and back to the beck.

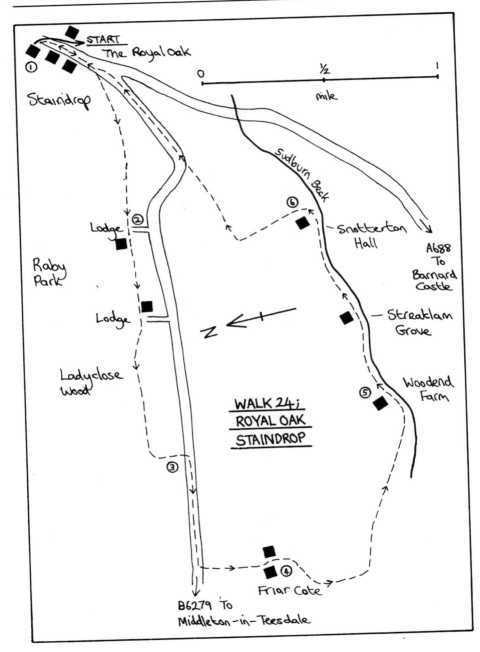

START
The Royal Oak

① Staindrop

0   ½   1
              mile

Sudburn Beck

Lodge ②

Raby Park

Lodge

Ladyclose Wood

N

⑥
Snotterton Hall

A688
To
Barnard
Castle

Streatlam Grove

⑤ Woodend Farm

WALK 24i
ROYAL OAK
STAINDROP

③

④
Friar Cote

B6279 To
Middleton-in-Teesdale

Pass over a farm drive and continue to a stile. Go through a gate to join a wooded path running beneath a canopy of beech trees. The Sudburn Beck is close by on the right. When you reach a footbridge over the beck swing left and head up the bank. At the top look for a gate at the corner of the wall. Bear left over a stile and then cross the paddock to reach a lane.

6. Follow Snotterton Lane as it bends to the right and runs straight to join the B6279 on a bend. Continue ahead, walking back into the centre of Staindrop.

The Royal Oak

25. Witton-le-Wear

Route: The Victoria Arms, Witton-le-Wear – Witton Castle – Witton Park – Escomb – Woodside – Witton Castle – The Victoria Arms, Witton-le-Wear

Distance: 6½ miles

Map: OS Pathfinder 580, OS Landranger 92

Start: The Victoria Arms, Witton-le-Wear. The inn is in the village centre, a few hundred yards from the A68, between Crook and Darlington.

Public transport: Local services, including routes 85 and 86.

The Victoria Arms, Witton-le-Wear (01388 488501)

A popular village local, there is also a strong family theme at the Victoria Arms, which is a Vaux pub. The inn was originally one of five inns in Witton-le-Wear. Food is available seven days a week, there is a children's menu and the permanent real ale on handpump is Vaux Bitter. Outside, the inn sign depicts a youthful-looking Queen Victoria. Times of opening are 11.00 – 3.00 and 6.00 – 11.00 from Monday to Friday, 11.00 – 11.00 on Saturday and 12.00 – 3.00 and 7.00 – 10.30 on Sunday.

The Victoria Arms

The Saxon Inn, Escomb (0388 662256)

Food is served every day at this popular village inn, which is on the Escomb church tourist trail. Boddingtons is the main brew and there is also a guest ale. Times of opening are 11.15 – 3.30 and 7.00 – 11.00 during the week and 12.00 – 3.00 and 7.00 – 10.30 on Sunday. However, opening times can vary.

Witton Castle

Erected by Ralph de Eure in the 15th century, medieval Witton Castle was largely rebuilt in later years following a terrible fire that caused extensive damage. Only the outer walls, tower house and turrets survived. You might not expect to find a 15th century castle playing host to holiday caravaners and campers but that is exactly what it does. Witton Castle opened as a holiday base in 1965 and in the first three months was visited by 50,000 people. There had never been anything like it before and certainly it was all a far cry from the traditional perception of a stately English monument. Enclosed by woods, the castle is best appreciated from the green at Witton-le-Wear.

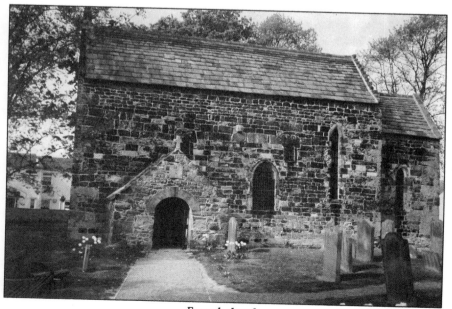

Escomb church

Escomb Church

Probably one of the most historic churches in the north-east, the Saxon church of St John the Evangelist is circumnavigated by a road serving a local housing estate. Nonetheless, it is a peaceful spot, the little church located amidst trees and ancient gravestones. The precise age of the church is not known but it is thought to date back to the 7th century and is one of the best examples of early Christian architecture in Northern Europe. The stones used in its construction come from the nearby Roman fort at Binchester. The church can be visited.

The Walk

1. Leave the inn, turn left and walk along the road. Various houses and cottages overlook a narrow triangular green in the centre of the village. The nearby church dates back to the 13th century and was rebuilt in 1902. Pass the community centre, then bear left and go down the hill. Pass under the old railway bridge on the line between Bishop Auckland and Eastgate and continue along the road. Cross the river Wear further on, wide at this point and fringed by trees. Just beyond it bear left into the grounds of Witton Castle, coinciding now with the Wear Valley Way.

2. Follow the drive through the woodland and then out across open parkland. Part of the castle can be glimpsed at this point. Just before the drive enters another burst of woodland, bear left through a gap in the wall. Follow the path to a junction, then turn right and soon a glorious reach of the Wear comes into view. On the opposite bank is the Low Barns Nature Reserve, haunt of waterfowl and woodland birds. The site includes 50 hectares of woods, lakes and meadow, a nature trail and a visitor centre. After only a few yards begin to veer away from the river and up the bank through the trees. Cross a field boundary and then continue to maintain the same direction with the unseen river down below you among the trees. Join a track and follow it to a gate and stile. In the next field continue in the same direction. A viaduct is visible ahead now. Keep to the track along the left-hand edge of the field, cross a stile by some gorse bushes and then you follow it round a left-hand bend. At the road turn right.

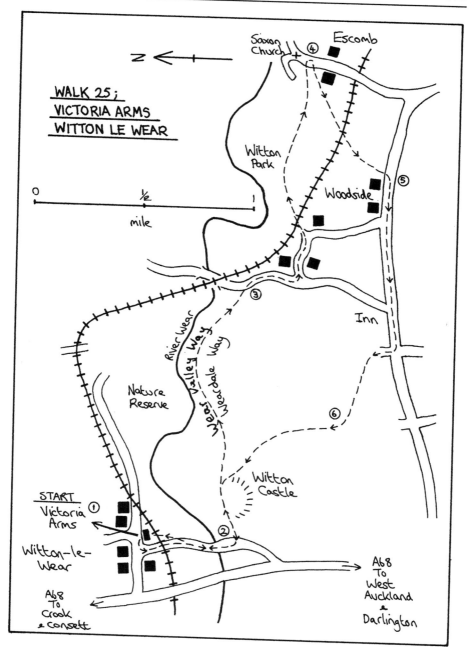

Z ←—┼———→

WALK 25;
VICTORIA ARMS
WITTON LE WEAR

0 ——————┼—————— ½
mile

Saxon Church ④ Escomb

Witton Park

Woodside ⑤

River Wear

③

Inn

Wear Valley Way

Weardale Way

Nature Reserve

⑥

Witton Castle

START
Victoria ①
Arms

Witton-le-
Wear

②

A68
To
Crook
& Consett

A68
To
West
Auckland
&
Darlington

3. Follow the pavement and pass the village sign for Witton Park, an old coal mining village. Follow the road as it bends sharp left, then turn left when the road swings right. Go under the railway bridge. The disused station at Witton Park is on the right. Beyond the bridge you come to a junction of tracks. Take the third from left and go up the slope and in front of you is the entrance to Northern Aggregates. Follow the path overlooking the valley and head towards Escomb. Cut between hedges and banks of undergrowth, cross several field boundaries and soon the buildings of Escomb come into view. Pass some allotments and join the road. Very quickly you reach the Saxon Inn and Escomb church opposite.

4. Retrace your steps back towards the allotments. Before you reach them, bear left at the end of the houses and go up the grassy slope. The houses are now on your left. At the top of the slope go through a gate, then turn right and walk alongside Escomb recreation area. Follow the track as it runs across the open ground. Turn left at some old dilapidated buildings, cross the railway line, swing right and follow a path running parallel to it. After about 150 yards veer left at a footbridge. Cross the field by heading diagonally right and cross into the next field. Maintain the same direction and head for some pylons and several houses. Look for a path here and follow it to the road.

5. Turn right and walk between rows of stone terraced houses. Pass a cemetery on your left and an inn, the Royal, on the right. There are pleasant rural views from this higher ground. Turn right at a farm, where there are 30 mile an hour speed restriction signs, and follow the track. Midway between the first farm and the second, there is a footpath on the left. Follow it between fences and after about 60 yards continue ahead with a wall on your right. Cross the field boundary and just before the corner cross a stone stile into the right-hand field. Swing left at once and continue to maintain the same direction. Cross the stile in the field corner and join a track.

6. Turn right and follow it between hedgerows. Soon you skirt the boundary wall of Witton Castle. Drop down the steep slope, cutting between beech trees, to meet the outward leg of the walk. Retrace your steps through the parkland, following the drive to the road. Turn right, cross the Wear and follow the road until it begins to curve left. Cross the stile on the right and bear left. Cross the field by keeping

parallel to the road and look for a gate in the boundary ahead, just to the right of a bungalow. Cross several greyhound enclosures and a stream, go up a flight of steps, cross the railway line and head up a steep path. At the top join the road, turn right and return to the inn.

NORTH PENNINES

England's Last Wilderness

For FREE
accommodation guide
and information pack
please telephone:

Alston Tourist
Information Centre
Tel: 01434 381696
or
Stanhope Tourist
Information Centre
Tel: 01388 527650

We can guarantee that, if you like peace and quiet with opportunities for walking, exploring, discovering interesting attractions and admiring local crafts, then we certainly have something for you!

We hope that you have enjoyed this book. Sigma Leisure publish a wide range of other titles, including general interest publications, guides to individual towns, and books for outdoor activities centred on walking and cycling in the great outdoors throughout England and Wales. This is a recent selection:

Country Walking . . .

50 CLASSIC WALKS IN THE PENNINES – Terry Marsh *(£8.95)*

WEST PENNINE WALKS – Mike Cresswell

RAMBLES IN NORTH WALES – Roger Redfern

EAST CHESHIRE WALKS – Graham Beech

WEST CHESHIRE WALKS – Jen Darling

STAFFORDSHIRE WALKS: Simply Superb – Les Lumsdon

NEWARK AND SHERWOOD RAMBLES – Malcolm McKenzie

NORTH NOTTINGHAMSHIRE RAMBLES – Malcolm McKenzie

RAMBLES AROUND NOTTINGHAM & DERBY – Keith Taylor

RAMBLES AROUND MANCHESTER – Mike Cresswell

HILL WALKS IN MID-WALES – David Ing

WELSH WALKS: Dolgellau & Cambrian Coast – L. Main and M. Perrott *(£5.95)*

WELSH WALKS: Aberystwyth and District – L. Main and M. Perrott*(£5.95)*

TEASHOP WALKS IN THE CHILTERNS – Jean Patefield

WATERWAY WALKS AROUND BIRMINGHAM – David Perrott

NORTH WEST WATERWAY WALKS: South of The Mersey – Guy Lawson

NORTH WEST WATERWAY WALKS: Mersey Waterways – David Parry

WALKING IN HAUNTED GLOUCESTERSHIRE – Florence Jackson & Gordon Ottewell

GLOUCESTERSHIRE HERITAGE WALKS – John Abbott

– all of the above books are currently £6.95 each, except where indicated

Lake District Walks . . .

LAKELAND ROCKY RAMBLES: Geology Beneath Your Feet – Bryan Lynas *(£9.95)*

FULL DAYS ON THE FELLS: 25 challenging walks – Adrian Dixon (Summer '95)

100 LAKE DISTRICT HILL WALKS – Gordon Brown *(£7.95)*

LAKELAND WALKING ON THE LEVEL – Norman Buckley *(£6.95)*

MOSTLY DOWNHILL IN THE LAKE DISTRICT – Alan Pears *(£6.95)*

Peak District Walks . . .

THE BOGTROTTER'S GUIDE ¬ Chris Holmes *(£6.95)*

HERITAGE WALKS IN THE PEAK DISTRICT – Clive Price *(£6.95)*

WALKING PEAKLAND TRACKWAYS – Mike Cresswell *(£7.95)*

MOSTLY DOWNHILL, Leisurely Walks – White Peak – Clive Price *(£6.95)*

MOSTLY DOWNHILL, Leisurely Walks – Dark Peak – Clive Price *(£6.95)*

TEASHOP WALKS IN THE PEAK DISTRICT – Clive Price *(£6.95)*

HALF-DAY WALKS IN THE PEAK DISTRICT – Alan Bradley *(£6.95)*

PEAKLAND RIVER VALLEY WALKS – Tony Stephens *(£6.95)*

Cycling with Sigma . . .

CYCLE UK! The Essential Guide to Leisure Cycling – Les Lumsdon *(£9.95)*

OFF-BEAT CYCLING & MOUNTAIN BIKING IN THE PEAK DISTRICT; MORE OFF-BEAT CYCLING IN THE PEAK DISTRICT – Clive Smith *(£6.95)* *each*

50 BEST CYCLE RIDES IN CHESHIRE – edited by Graham Beech *(£7.95)*

CYCLING IN THE LAKE DISTRICT – John Wood *(£7.95)*

CYCLING IN SOUTH WALES – Rosemary Evans *(£7.95)*

CYCLING IN THE COTSWOLDS – Stephen Hill *(£7.95)*

CYCLING IN STAFFORDSHIRE – Linda Wain *(£7.95)*

CYCLING IN THE WEST COUNTRY – Helen Stephenson *(£7.95)*

CYCLING IN SCOTLAND AND NE ENGLAND – Philip Routledge *(£7.95)*

BY-WAY BIKING IN THE CHILTERNS – Henry Tindell *(£7.95)*

Long-distance & Challenge Walks . . .

CHALLENGING WALKS IN NORTH-WEST BRITAIN – Ron Astley (£7.95)

THE GREATER MANCHESTER BOUNDARY WALK – Graham Phythian

THE THIRLMERE WAY – Tim Cappelli

THE FURNESS TRAIL – Tim Cappelli

THE MARCHES WAY – Les Lumsdon

THE TWO ROSES WAY – Peter Billington, et al

THE RED ROSE WALK – Tom Schofield

FROM WHARFEDALE TO WESTMORLAND: historical walks through the Yorkshire Dales – Aline Watson

THE WEST YORKSHIRE WAY – Nicholas Parrott

– all £6.95 each except where indicated

The Best Pub Walks!

Sigma publish the widest range of "Pub Walks" guides, covering just about every popular walking destination in England and Wales. Each book includes 25 – 30 interesting walks and varied suitable for individuals or family groups. The walks are based on "Real Ale" inns of character and are all accessible by public transport.
Areas covered include

Cheshire • Dartmoor • Exmoor • Isle of Wight • Yorkshire Dales • Peak District • Pennines • Lake District • Cotswolds • Mendips • Cornwall • Lancashire • Oxfordshire • Snowdonia • Devon • Northumbria • Snowdonia • Manchester
... and dozens more – all £6.95 each!

General interest . . .

TRAINING THE LEARNER DRIVER: The Key to Success in Passing the Test! – Don L Gates. Learn how to teach the skills of driving, possibly without expensive driving school lessons. Clearly illustrated. (£6.95)

THE INCREDIBLY BIASED BEER GUIDE – Ruth Herman. All that's best about Britain's small brewers. (£6.95)

DIAL 999 – EMERGENCY SERVICES IN ACTION – John Creighton. Colour and black and white photographs illustrate this dramatic book. (£6.95)

THE ALABAMA AFFAIR – David Hollett. Tales of subterfuge in the American Civil war that make today's politicians look like angels! (£6.95)

PEAK DISTRICT DIARY – Roger Redfern: an evocative collection of photographs by a Guardian contributor. *(£6.95)*

I REMAIN, YOUR SON JACK – J. C. Morten (edited by Sheila Morten): A collection of almost 200 letters, as featured on BBC TV, telling the moving story of a young soldier in the First World War. *(£8.95)*

FORGOTTEN DIVISIONS – John Fox. A unique account of the 1914 – 18 War, drawing on the experience of soldiers and civilians, from a Lancashire town and a Rhineland village. *(£7.95)*

ROAD SENSE – Doug Holland. A book for drivers with some experience, preparing them for an advanced driving test. The book introduces a recommended system of car control, based on that developed by the Police Driving School. *(£5.95)*

WE ALSO PUBLISH:

A series of investigations into the Supernatural, Myth and Magic:

GHOSTS, TRADITIONS AND LEGENDS OF OLD LANCASHIRE – Ken Howarth *(£7.95)*

SHADOWS: A northern investigation of the unknown – Steve Cliffe *(£7.95)*

MYSTERIES OF THE MERSEY VALLEY– Jenny Randles and Peter Hough *(£7.95)*

Superb illustrated books on Manchester's football teams:

UNITED WE STOOD – the unofficial history of the Ferguson Years – Richard Kurt. *(£6.95)*

RED FEVER! From Rochdale to Rio as United Supporters – Steve Donoghue. *(£7.95)*

MANCHESTER CITY, Moments to Remember – John Creighton. *(£9.95)*

Many more entertaining and educational books are being regularly added to our list. All of our books are available from your local bookshop. In case of difficulty, or to obtain our complete catalogue, please contact:

Sigma Leisure,1 South Oak Lane, Wilmslow, Cheshire SK9 6AR

Phone: 01625 – 531035. Fax: 01625 – 536800

ACCESS and VISA orders welcome – call our friendly sales staff or use our 24 hour Answerphone service! Most orders are despatched on the day we receive your order – you could be enjoying our books in just a couple of days.